Microsoft® Excel®
2010

PowerPivot

Microsoft® Excel® 2010: PowerPivot

Part Number: 084606
Course Edition: 1.0

NOTICES

HELP US IMPROVE OUR COURSEWARE

Your comments are important to us. Please contact us at Element K Press LLC, 1-800-478-7788, 500 Canal View Boulevard, Rochester, NY 14623, Attention: Product Planning, or through our Web site at **http://support.elementkcourseware.com**.

Microsoft® Excel® 2010: PowerPivot

e.g. Sums at different lines *calculated fields* (handwritten annotation)

About This Course

Your training in *Microsoft® Excel® 2010* has provided you with a solid foundation in the basic and intermediate skills for using the software. You may have used Excel to enter and store large amounts of data, and now you may want to enhance your skill of analyzing data by importing data from various sources. In this course, you will use Microsoft Excel 2010's PowerPivot add-in, which will help you in performing better data analysis.

As your business expands, you may need to keep stock of a large volume of data, but Excel cannot handle data beyond a certain row limit. PowerPivot lets you import large volumes of data, and also provides you with the added advantage of importing data from various sources. PowerPivot provides you with interactive reporting tools, including DAX functions, which will help you to create dynamic reports and arrive at clear and concise conclusions.

Course Description

Target Student

This course is for students with a sound working knowledge of Microsoft Excel 2010 and general computing proficiency, including those who will be using Excel to make business decisions.

Course Prerequisites

To ensure your success, we recommend you first take one of the following Element K courses or have equivalent knowledge: *Microsoft® Excel® 2010: Level 1, Microsoft® Excel® 2010: Level 2,* and *Microsoft® Excel® 2010: Level 3.*

Course Objectives

In this course, you will make use of the PowerPivot add-in to import data from various sources and create a dynamic report.

You will:

* Become familiar with the PowerPivot application and import data.

* Manipulate data in a PowerPivot worksheet.

* Create reports using PowerPivot data.

- Use DAX functions in PowerPivot.
- Distribute PowerPivot Data.

How to Use This Book

As a Learning Guide

This book is divided into lessons and topics, covering a subject or a set of related subjects. In most cases, lessons are arranged in order of increasing proficiency.

The results-oriented topics include relevant and supporting information you need to master the content. Each topic has various types of activities designed to enable you to practice the guidelines and procedures as well as to solidify your understanding of the informational material presented in the course.

At the back of the book, you will find a glossary of the definitions of the terms and concepts used throughout the course. You will also find an index to assist in locating information within the instructional components of the book.

In the Classroom

This book is intended to enhance and support the in-class experience. Procedures and guidelines are presented in a concise fashion along with activities and discussions. Information is provided for reference and reflection in such a way as to facilitate understanding and practice.

Each lesson may also include a Lesson Lab or various types of simulated activities. You will find the files for the simulated activities along with the other course files on the enclosed CD-ROM. If your course manual did not come with a CD-ROM, please go to **http://www.elementk.com/courseware-file-downloads** to download the files. If included, these interactive activities enable you to practice your skills in an immersive business environment, or to use hardware and software resources not available in the classroom. The course files that are available on the CD-ROM or by download may also contain sample files, support files, and additional reference materials for use both during and after the course.

As a Teaching Guide

Effective presentation of the information and skills contained in this book requires adequate preparation. As such, as an instructor, you should familiarize yourself with the content of the entire course, including its organization and approaches. You should review each of the student activities and exercises so you can facilitate them in the classroom.

Throughout the book, you may see Instructor Notes that provide suggestions, answers to problems, and supplemental information for you, the instructor. You may also see references to "Additional Instructor Notes" that contain expanded instructional information; these notes appear in a separate section at the back of the book. PowerPoint slides may be provided on the included course files, which are available on the enclosed CD-ROM or by download from http://www.elementk.com/courseware-file-downloads. The slides are also referred to in the text. If you plan to use the slides, it is recommended to display them during the corresponding content as indicated in the instructor notes in the margin.

The course files may also include assessments for the course, which can be administered diagnostically before the class, or as a review after the course is completed. These exam-type questions can be used to gauge the students' understanding and assimilation of course content.

As a Review Tool

Any method of instruction is only as effective as the time and effort you, the student, are willing to invest in it. In addition, some of the information that you learn in class may not be important to you immediately, but it may become important later. For this reason, we encourage you to spend some time reviewing the content of the course after your time in the classroom.

As a Reference

The organization and layout of this book make it an easy-to-use resource for future reference. Taking advantage of the glossary, index, and table of contents, you can use this book as a first source of definitions, background information, and summaries.

Course Icons

Icon	Description
	A **Caution Note** makes students aware of potential negative consequences of an action, setting, or decision that are not easily known.
	Display Slide provides a prompt to the instructor to display a specific slide. Display Slides are included in the Instructor Guide only.
	An **Instructor Note** is a comment to the instructor regarding delivery, classroom strategy, classroom tools, exceptions, and other special considerations. Instructor Notes are included in the Instructor Guide only.
	Notes Page indicates a page that has been left intentionally blank for students to write on.
	A **Student Note** provides additional information, guidance, or hints about a topic or task.
	A **Version Note** indicates information necessary for a specific version of software.

Course Requirements

Hardware

For this course, you will need one computer for each student and one for the instructor. Each computer will require the following minimum hardware configuration:

- A PC with a Pentium® processor, at least 300 MHz.
- 10 GB of hard disk space or larger. You should have at least 1 GB of free hard disk space available for Office installation.
- A minimum of 64 MB of RAM with 1 GB of free hard disk space.
- A CD-ROM drive.
- Keyboard and mouse or other pointing device.
- 1024 x 768 resolution monitor is recommended.
- Network cards and cabling for local network access.
- Internet access (contact your local network administrator).
- A printer (optional) or an installed printer driver.

- A projection system to display the instructor's computer screen.

Software

A licensed copy of the following software for the instructor and each student:

- Microsoft® Office Professional Plus 2010 Edition
- Microsoft® Windows 7 (Professional Edition)
- PowerPivot for Excel
- Adobe® Reader®

Class Setup

For Instructor and Student Desktop Operating System Installation

1. Make sure that all computer components are properly installed and working.

2. Perform a fresh installation of Windows 7 Professional. You can boot the computer from the installation DVD-ROM, or create a network boot disk and install from a network share. After you configure the first computer of each type, you might wish to create a ghost image and install that to the remaining classroom computers. Regardless of your installation method, use the following installation parameters:

    a. In the Install Windows window, accept the default values to set **Language to install** to **English, Time and currency format** to **English (United States), Keyboard or input method** to **US.** Click **Next.**

    b. Click **Install now.**

    c. Accept the license terms and click **Next** to continue.

    d. On the **Which type of installation do you want** screen, select **Custom (Advanced).**

    e. In the **Where do you want to install Windows** window, select **Drive options (advanced).** Delete the existing partitions and create a primary partition with a capacity of 20 GB (40960). Leave the remaining as unallocated free space. Format the partition to NTFS.

    f. Verify that the primary partition is selected and click **Next** to continue.

    g. The computer will automatically restart after a few minutes. Remove the DVD before the system restarts.

    h. In the **Type a user name (for example, John)** text box, enter *Admin##*, where *##* is a unique two-digit number assigned to each student. Name the instructor's user account *Admin.* This account will become a member of the local Administrators group by default.

    i. In the **Type a computer name** text box, type a computer name. For the instructor's computer, name the computer *INST*

    j. For student computers, name each one *Client##*, where *##* is a unique two-digit number assigned to each student.

    k. Click **Next** to continue.

    l. In the **Type a password (recommended)** text box, type *!Pass1234*

    m. In the **Retype your password** text box, type *!Pass1234*

    n. In the **Type a password hint** text box, type *!Pass1234* and click **Next** to continue.

o. In the **Product key (dashes will be added automatically)** text box, type the product key of your software, verify that the **Automatically activate Windows when I'm online** check box is checked and then click **Next** to continue.

p. On the **Help protect your computer and improve Windows automatically** screen, click **Use recommended settings.**

q. Specify your time and date settings.

  ■ From the **Time Zone** drop-down list, select your time zone.

  ■ In the **Date** section, select the date.

  ■ If necessary, modify the system time.

r. Click **Next** to continue.

s. On the **Select your computer's current location** screen, click **Work.**

3. On the computer, install a printer driver (a physical print device is optional). Click **Start** and choose **Printers and Faxes.** Under **Printer Tasks**, click **Add a Printer** and follow the prompts.

  If you do not have a physical printer installed, right-click the printer and choose **Pause Printing** to prevent any print error message.

4. Perform a complete installation of Microsoft Office Professional 2010.

5. In the **User Name** dialog box, click **OK** to accept the default user name and initials.

6. In the **Microsoft Office 2010 Activation Wizard** dialog box, click **Next** to activate the Office 2010 application.

7. When the activation of Microsoft Office 2010 is complete, click **Close** to close the **Microsoft Office 2010 Activation Wizard** dialog box.

8. In the **User Name** dialog box, click **OK.**

9. In the **Welcome To Microsoft 2010** dialog box, click **Finish.** You must have an active Internet connection in order to complete this step. Here, you have to select the **Download And Install Updates From Microsoft Update When Available (Recommended)** option, so that whenever there is a new update, it gets automatically installed on your system.

10. After the Microsoft Update runs, in the **Microsoft Office** dialog box, click **OK.**

11. Install the PowerPivot add-in.

a. Go to the Microsoft website.

b. Install the 32-bit version by clicking the **Download** button.

c. Double-click the .msi file to start the **Setup** wizard

d. Click **Next** to start with the installation process.

e. Accept the licence agreement, and click **Next.**

f. In the **Name** text box, enter your name, and then click **Next.**

g. Click **Install,** and then click **Finish.**

12. Install Adobe reader.

13. On the course CD-ROM, open the 084606 folder. Then, open the Data folder. Run the 084606dd.exe self-extracting file located in it. This will install a folder named 084606Data on your C drive. This folder contains all the data files that you will use to complete this course. If your course did not come with a CD, please go to **http:// elementkcourseware.com** to download the data files.

Within each lesson folder, you may find a Solution folder. This folder contains solution files for the lesson's activities and lesson lab, which can be used by students to check their end results.

14. If necessary, minimize the **Language** bar.

15. Run the **Internet Connection Wizard** to set up the Internet connection as appropriate for your environment if you did not do so during installation.

16. Display known file type extensions.

    a. Right-click Start and then select **Open Windows Explorer.**

    b. In the Windows Explorer, click the **Organize** drop-down arrow, and select **Folder and search options.**

    c. In the **Folder Options** dialog box, select the **View** tab.

    d. In the **Advanced settings** list box, in the **Hidden files and folders** section, uncheck the **Hide extensions for known file types** check box.

    e. Click **OK** to close the **Folder Options** dialog box, and then close the Windows Explorer window.

Before Every Class

1. Log on to the computer as the Administrator user.

2. Delete any existing data file from the C:\084606Data folder.

3. Extract a fresh copy of the course data files from the CD-ROM provided with the course manual, or download the data files from **http://elementkcourseware.com.**

List of Additional Files

Printed with each activity is a list of files students open to complete that activity. Many activities also require additional files that students do not open, but are needed to support the file(s) students are working with. These supporting files are included with the student data files on the course CD-ROM or data disk. Do not delete these files.

1

Getting Started with PowerPivot

[handwritten: → needs to be installed 2010 Add-In to download from MS → Options /Add-Ins. Manage ____ [Com Add-ins]]

Lesson Time: 1 hour(s), 15 minutes

Lesson Objectives:

In this lesson, you will become familiar with the PowerPivot application and import data.

[handwritten: → If disappear Open 2 Close or Download fix from MSofr.]

You will:

- Identify the elements of the PowerPivot interface.

- Import data from various data sources.

- Refresh data from a data source.

- Create a linked table.

Introduction

You have used Microsoft Excel 2010 to enter and store large amounts of data. You may now want to use the data by performing advanced data mining and analysis with the PowerPivot add-in. In this lesson, you will identify the basic features and tools of PowerPivot.

Though PowerPivot is an Excel 2010 add-in, its interface includes components that are different from those in Excel. Moreover, it provides unique data handling functionality and also serves as a powerful analysis tool. Gaining familiarity with the PowerPivot interface and importing data into PowerPivot will set you on the path towards becoming proficient with the application.

[handwritten: PowerPivot v1 → Manual 2010 (2008 add-in) we are usn v2 → SQL 2012 version, installed v3 → only available in Professional right version ICP1 not available in v1]

TOPIC A

Explore the PowerPivot Application

Working with any new application requires that you become familiar with its interface. Similarly, before you start working with PowerPivot, you need to be aware of the various components present on the interface. In this topic, you will identify the elements of the PowerPivot user interface.

While working with a new application, you might waste a significant amount of time searching for specific options in the work environment. You can prevent this by familiarizing yourself with the elements of the user interface. This will help you to achieve the output that you are seeking when you work with the software.

PowerPivot

PowerPivot is an Excel add-in used for importing data from various sources and analyzing data using PivotTables and PivotCharts. PowerPivot allows you to integrate data from multiple sources and manipulate large data sets with ease. Using PowerPivot, you can manipulate more rows than the one million row limit in Excel; however, you cannot edit or enter any data in the PowerPivot window. You have to switch to the source application to edit imported data. PowerPivot data is saved in the Excel format and can be opened only in Excel; however, the data is not visible in an Excel workbook.

The PowerPivot Window

The PowerPivot application window displays components that enable you to work effectively and efficiently with data. *Diagram View v2.*

To build data set

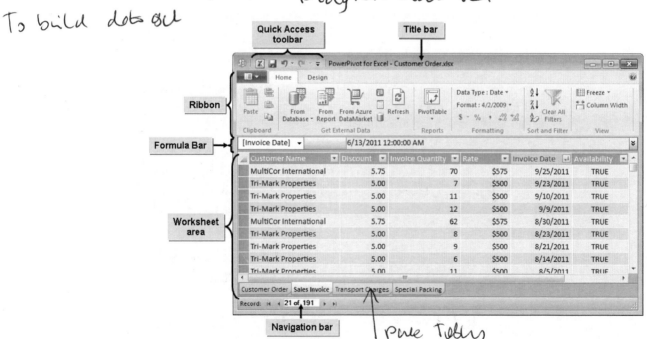

Figure 1-1: Components of the PowerPivot Window.

Component	Description
Title bar	A bar located at the top of the interface that displays the name of the file that you are currently working on.
Quick Access toolbar	A toolbar located adjacent to the title bar that provides easy access to frequently used commands.
Ribbon	A panel located below the Quick Access toolbar that displays commands relevant to a particular set of tasks. These commands are organized into different tabs and groups.
Formula Bar	A bar located below the Ribbon that displays the contents of the selected cell in a worksheet. It also displays the active column.
Worksheet area	An area located below the Formula Bar where the data is displayed as a worksheet.
Navigation bar	A bar located below the worksheet that allows you to navigate through the records in a worksheet.

The PowerPivot Ribbon

The PowerPivot Ribbon provides users with access to advanced data manipulation and analysis tools. The commands are categorized under different tabs.

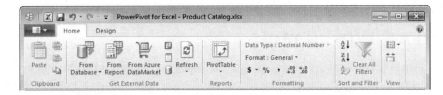

Figure 1-2: The Home tab of the PowerPivot window.

Figure 1-3: The Design tab of the PowerPivot window.

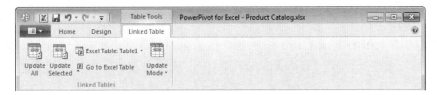

Figure 1-4: The Linked Table tab of the PowerPivot window.

Tab	Description
Home	Provides options to import data from various sources, create reports, sort and filter data, and set the data type.
Design	Provides options to manage table relationships, edit table properties, set the calculation mode, manipulate connections, and customize columns.
Linked Table	Provides options to update a table, navigate to the Excel worksheet, and set the mode in which you want it to be updated. This tab appears only when you select a table that is linked to an Excel table.

The PowerPivot Tab in Excel

The **PowerPivot** tab on the Excel Ribbon enables you to launch the PowerPivot window. It provides you with options to create new reports, create and manage measures, link a table, and set options for automatic detection of relationships in a field list.

Figure 1-5: *Options on the PowerPivot tab in Excel.*

PowerPivot Worksheets

A PowerPivot worksheet is an electronic spreadsheet used for storing imported data. The worksheet displays the data but cannot be edited. A PowerPivot worksheet can contain different types of data such as text, decimal numbers, whole numbers, currency, date, and boolean functions. Every worksheet has a name, which is displayed on the sheet tab bar below the worksheet. You can rename, delete, or reorder a worksheet.

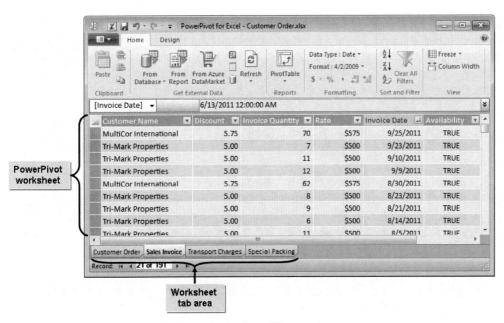

Figure 1-6: A PowerPivot worksheet displaying different data types.

ACTIVITY 1-1
Exploring the Options in the PowerPivot Interface

Data Files:

C:\084606Data\Getting Started With PowerPivot\Shipping.xlsx

Scenario:

You have been taking care of your company's business records for a couple of years using Microsoft Excel. Now that you have been promoted as a Business Analyst, you want to get into some serious data analysis. You have installed the PowerPivot add-in to help you in performing advanced data analysis. Because you are not familiar with the PowerPivot interface, you decide to spend some time to familiarize yourself with the options available on it.

1. Open the PowerPivot window.

   a. Click **Start→ All Programs→ Microsoft Office→ Microsoft Excel 2010.**

   b. In the **Microsoft Office Customization Installer** dialog box, click **Install.**

   c. Select the **File** tab, and choose **Open.**

   d. In the **Open** dialog box, navigate to the C:\084606Data\Getting Started with PowerPivot folder.

   e. Select the **Shipping.xlsx** file and click **Open.**

   f. On the Ribbon, select the **PowerPivot** tab, and in the **Launch** group, click **PowerPivot Window.**

   g. Maximize the PowerPivot window.

2. Explore the options in the PowerPivot Ribbon.

   a. Observe the various options available on the **Home** tab.

   b. Select the **Design** tab.

   c. Observe the various options available on the **Design** tab.

d.   Select the File tab, and observe the options available on it.

e.   Select the File tab again to hide the available options.

3.   Explore the PowerPivot interface.

a.   On the PowerPivot worksheet, select the second cell in the Country column.

b.   Observe that the text in the cell is also displayed in the Formula Bar.

c.   Below the worksheet area, on the sheet tab bar, select the **Product List** tab to display the data in the worksheet.

d.   At the left of the Formula Bar, click the Name Box drop-down arrow, and select **[Unit Price]** to select the first value in the Unit Price column.

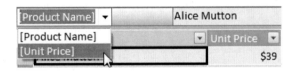   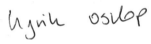

e.   On the Navigation bar, observe that **1 of 77** is displayed because the first value is selected, and click the first right arrow button, to navigate to the next record.

f.   On the Navigation bar, observe that **2 of 77** is displayed, and click the second right arrow button, to navigate to the last record.

g. Click at the left of the last row to select the entire record.

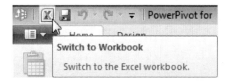

4. Display the PowerPivot help window.

   a. In the top right corner of the Ribbon, click the Help button.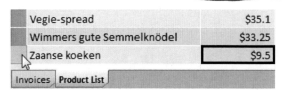

   b. Maximize the SQL Server PowerPivot for Microsoft Excel Help window.

   c. In the SQL Server PowerPivot for Microsoft Excel Help window, in the right pane, in the **Getting Started** section, click the **Take a Tour of the PowerPivot UI** link.

   ### ⊟ Getting Started

   We recommend that you read the following topic content.

   - Install PowerPivot for Excel
   - Learn About PowerPivot Capabilities
   - Take a Tour of the PowerPivot UI

   d. Scroll down, and observe the contents, and then close the SQL Server PowerPivot for Microsoft Excel Help window.

5. Close the Excel workbook.

   a. In the PowerPivot window, on the Quick Access toolbar, click the **Switch to Workbook** button.

   b. In the Excel window, on the top right corner, click the **Close Window** button.

   c. If necessary, in the **Microsoft Excel** message box, click **Don't Save** to close the file without saving any changes.

TOPIC B

Import Data from Various Data Sources

You explored the PowerPivot user interface. The first step toward data analysis using PowerPivot is to import data into PowerPivot. In this topic, you will import data from various data sources.

Excel's PowerPivot add-in helps you to analyze large volumes of data with ease. However, your work may often require you to analyze data that is created using other applications. It can be tedious analyzing such data if you are not familiar with the application that the data is native to. In such cases, you can import the data and then use PowerPivot's features to work with it.

PowerPivot Data Sources

PowerPivot allows you to import data from numerous data sources. The data sources can be broadly classified into four categories.

Data Source Category	*Description*
Relational databases	PowerPivot allows you to import data from various relational databases. You can import tables or views from the database or use data returned from a query.
Multidimensional sources	PowerPivot creates a connection with a SQL Server Analysis Services cube, and then imports the data returned by a multidimensional expression query.
Data feeds	PowerPivot creates a connection with various data feeds, such as Microsoft Reporting Services reports and Azure DataMarket data sets, and then imports data.
Text files	PowerPivot enables you to import data from text files and Excel worksheets.

Relational Database Formats Supported in PowerPivot

Data can be imported from different types of relational databases. PowerPivot provides you with support for various versions of each relational database.

Relational Database	*Versions*
Microsoft SQL Server	Microsoft SQL Server2005, 2008, 2008 R2; Microsoft SQL Azure Database; SQL Server Parallel Data Warehouse
Oracle	Oracle 9i, 10g, 11g
Teradata	Teradata V2R6, V12
IBM DB2	8.1

PowerPivot also allows users to import data from other relational databases such as Informix, Sybase, and other data sources by using an OLE DB provider or OLE DB for ODBC provider.

Data Feeds

Definition:

A *data feed* is a mechanism that enables you to receive updated data from a subscribed data source. It provides data in a structured format. Data from a data feed can be received and converted to a format that is usable. Such data is usually stored in a file format, such as CSV or XML, which also defines the structure.

Example:

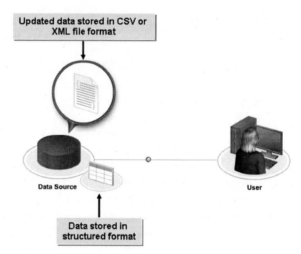

Figure 1-7: *A representation of the data feed mechanism.*

The Table Import Wizard

The **Table Import Wizard** allows you to perform a step-by-step import of data from various sources, such as relational databases, multidimensional sources, data feeds, and text files. Depending on the data source, the wizard provides advanced options to select the data that you want to import. You can also test the connectivity with the data source.

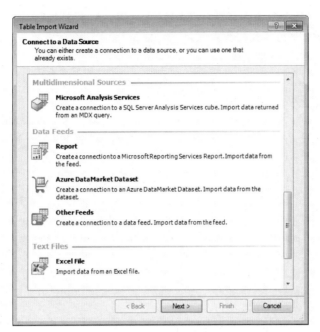

Figure 1-8: The Table Import Wizard displaying data sources from which data can be imported.

Data Types

When you import data, it is stored automatically in one of the data types supported by PowerPivot.

Data Type	Description
Whole Number	Numbers that do not have decimal places. Numbers can be negative or positive.
Decimal Number	A real number that may have any number of digits after the decimal point.
TRUE/FALSE	A true or false value represented by either 1 or 0.
Text	A string of character data comprised of alphabets, numbers, and other characters. Numbers and dates can also be represented in a text format.
Date	Dates and times in appropriate date-time representations.
Currency	Numeric values that represent currency.

How to Import Data from Various Data Sources

Procedure Reference: Import Data from a Text File

To import a data from a text file:

1. In the Excel window, on the **PowerPivot** tab, in the **Launch** group, click **PowerPivot Window** to display the PowerPivot window.

2. In the PowerPivot window, on the **Home** tab, in the **Get External Data** group, click a button to launch the **Table Import Wizard** for importing data from a text file.

   ● Click **From Text.**

   ● Click **From Other Sources.**

3. If necessary, in the Table Import Wizard, in the **Connect to a Data Source** page, in the list box, in the **Text Files** section, select **Text File** and then click **Next.**

4. In the **Table Import Wizard,** in the **Connect to a Flat File** page, in the **Friendly connection name** text box, enter a name for the connection.

5. In the **File Path** text box, type a file name with its complete path; or click **Browse,** and in the **Open** dialog box, navigate to the folder containing the desired text file, select the file, and then click **Open.**

6. From the **Column Separator** drop-down list, select an option to specify the character that separates data values in the text file.

7. If necessary, click **Advanced,** and in the **Advanced Settings** dialog box, set the **Encoding** and **Locale** options, and then click **OK.**

8. If necessary, check the **Use first row as column headers** check box to specify that the first row of data in the text file contains column headers.

9. If necessary, click **Clear Row Filters** to clear the filters applied to the data.

10. Click **Finish** to start the importing process.

11. In the **Table Import Wizard,** in the **Importing** page, click **Close** to close the wizard.

Procedure Reference: Import Data from an Access Database

To import data from an Access database:

1. In the Excel window, on the **PowerPivot** tab, in the **Launch** group, click **PowerPivot Window** to display the PowerPivot window.

2. In the PowerPivot window, on the **Home** tab, in the **Get External Data** group, select an option to launch the **Table Import Wizard** for importing data from a text file.

   ● From the **From Database** drop-down list, select **From Access.**

   ● Click **From Other Sources.**

3. If necessary, in the Table Import Wizard, in the **Connect to a Data Source** page, in the list box, in the **Relational Databases** section, select **Microsoft Access,** and then click **Next.**

4. In the **Table Import Wizard,** in the **Connect to a Microsoft Access Database** page, in the **Friendly connection name** text box, enter a name for the connection.

5. In the **Database name** text box, type a database name with its complete path; or click **Browse,** and in the **Open** dialog box, navigate to the folder containing the desired Access database, select the database, and then click **Open.**

6. If necessary, in the **User name** and **Password** text box, enter the login credentials for the database, and check the **Save my password** check box.

7. If necessary, click **Advanced,** and in the **Advanced** dialog box, select a provider and set the connection string properties, and then click **OK.**

8. Click **Test Connection,** to check the connection with the Access database, and in the **PowerPivot for Excel** message box, click **OK.**

9. In the **Connect to a Microsoft Access Database** page, click **Next.**

10. Specify the data source.

   ● Import the data from a table or view.

      a. In the **Choose How to Import the Data** page, select the **Select from a list of tables and views to choose the data to import** option, and then click **Next.**

      b. In the **Select Tables and Views** page, in the **Tables and Views** section, select the desired tables to be imported.

      c. If necessary, click **Preview & Filter** to view the table data and apply filters to it, and then click **OK.**

      d. Click **Finish** to start the importing process.

      e. Click **Close** to close the **Table Import Wizard.**

   ● Write a query to specify the data to be imported.

      a. Select the **Write a query that will specify the data to import** option, and in the **Specify a SQL Query** page, in the **SQL Statement** text box, enter a valid query.

      b. Click **Validate,** to check the validity of the SQL statement.

      c. Click **Design,** and in the **Table Import Wizard,** build the query statement, and then click **OK.**

      d. Click **Finish** to start the importing process, and then click **Close** to close the **Table Import Wizard.**

Procedure Reference: Import Data from Data Feeds

To import data from data feeds:

1. In the PowerPivot window, on the **Home** tab, in the **Get External Data** group, select an option to launch the **Table Import Wizard** for importing data from a data feed.

   ● On the **Home** tab, in the **Get External Data** group, click **From Data Feeds.**

   ● On the **Home** tab, in the **Get External Data** group, click **From Other Data Sources.**

2. In the **Friendly connection name** text box, specify a name for the connection.

3. In the **Table Import Wizard,** in the **Connect to a Data Feed** page, in the **Data Feed Url** text box, enter the url of the data feed.

4. If necessary, click **Advanced,** and in the **Advanced** dialog box, select a provider and set the connection string properties, and then click **OK.**

5. Click **Test Connection** to ensure that the feed is available.

6. Click **Next** to continue with the importing process.

7. In the **Select Tables and Views** page, in the **Tables and Views** section, select the tables in the data feed that need to be imported.

8. Click **Preview & Filter** to preview the data and change the column sections, and then click **OK.**

9. In the **Select Tables and Views** page, click **Finish.**

10. In the **Importing** page, click **Close** to finish the importing process.

Procedure Reference: Copy and Paste Data into a New Table

To copy and paste data into a new table:

1. In the Excel window, select the range of data that is to be copied.

2. On the **Home** tab, in the **Clipboard** group, click **Copy.**

3. Select the **PowerPivot** tab, and in the **Launch** group, click **PowerPivot Window** to display the PowerPivot window.

4. In the PowerPivot window, on the **Home** tab, in the **Clipboard** group, select a paste option.

   - Click **Paste** to paste the contents of the clipboard into a new table in the PowerPivot window.

   - Click **Paste Append** to paste the contents of the clipboard into an existing table.

   - Click **Paste Replace** to replace the existing table with the contents in the clipboard.

5. If necessary, in the **Paste Preview** dialog box, in the **Table Name** text box, enter a name for the table, and if necessary, set the first row to appear as the column header by checking the **Use first row as column headers** check box, and then click **OK.**

Restrictions when Pasting Data

The **Paste Append** and **Paste Replace** options are available only when you are working with a table that was created by pasting data into the clipboard. When you paste data using these options, the new data must have the same number of columns as the old data. It is preferable to paste columns of data that are of the same data type as that in the destination table. You can also use a different data type, but it will generally display a Type Mismatch error.

ACTIVITY 1-2
Importing Data from an Access Database

Data Files:

C:\084606Data\Getting Started With PowerPivot\Customer Order.accdb

Before You Begin:
The Excel application is open.

Scenario:
Your boss wants you to analyze the changing trends in the orders placed by a few customers. He has given you an Access database, which contains details of the invoices made to customers against orders placed by them. You are also told that the sales details were being updated and the database may not have the updated sales information. You decide to import the other information and await confirmation regarding the sales details.

---

1. Select the database to be imported.

    a. In the Excel window, select the **File** tab, and choose **New.**

    b. In the **Available Templates** section, double-click **Blank workbook.**

    c. On the **PowerPivot** tab, in the **Launch** group, click **PowerPivot Window.**

    d. In the PowerPivot window, on the **Home** tab, in the **Get External Data** group, from the **From Database** drop-down list, select **From Access.**

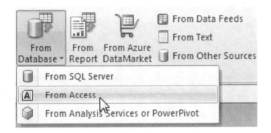

    e. In the **Table Import Wizard,** in the **Connect to a Microsoft Access Database** page, click **Browse.**

    f. In the **Open** dialog box, verify that the C:\084606Data\Getting Started with PowerPivot folder is selected, select the **Customer Order.accdb** file, and then click **Open.**

---

2. Test the connectivity with the Access database.

a.   In the **Friendly connection name** text box, observe that the connection name is displayed as **Access Customer Order.**

(handwritten note in left margin: bug? import)

b.   Click **Test Connection.**

c.   In the **PowerPivot for Excel** message box, observe the message that the connection has succeeded, and click **OK.**

3.   Import the Access data into the PowerPivot window.

a.   In the **Table Import Wizard,** in the **Connect to a Microsoft Access Database** page, click **Next.**

b.   In the **Choose How to Import the Data** page, verify that the **Select from a list of tables and views to choose the data to import** option is selected, and click **Next.**

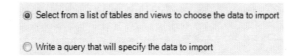

c.   In the **Select Tables and Views** page, in the **Tables and Views** section, check the **tblCustomer** check box, and then click on the **Friendly Name** column.

d.   Double-click to select the existing text, type *Customer Order* and then press **Enter.**

e.   Check the **tblTransport** check box, and then click on the **Friendly Name** column.

f.   Double-click to select the existing text, type *Transport Charges* and press **Enter.**

g.   Click **Finish** to start the importing.

h.   In the **Importing** page, observe that both the tables have been successfully imported, and then click **Close** to close the **Table Import Wizard.**

i.   In the PowerPivot window, observe that both the worksheets have been imported as separate worksheets.

4.   Save the worksheet.

a.   On the Quick Access toolbar, click the **Save** button.

b.   In the **Save As** dialog box, verify that the C:\084606Data\Getting Started with PowerPivot folder is selected.

c.   In the **File name** text box, type *My Customer Order* and click **Save.**

d.   In the top right corner of the workbook window, click the **Close Window** button.

ACTIVITY 1-3
Importing Data from a Text File

Data Files:

C:\084606Data\Getting Started With PowerPivot\Order Details.txt

Before You Begin:

The Excel application is open.

Scenario:

A colleague and you are responsible for analyzing a division's order details of the past six months. Your colleague, who took the responsibility for collecting the details, informs you that the data is in a text file format. You decide to use PowerPivot to proceed with the data analysis.

---

1. Open a new worksheet.

   a. In the Excel window, select the **File** tab, and choose **New.**

   b. In the Backstage view, in the **Available Templates** section, double-click **Blank workbook.**

---

2. Import the data from the text file.

   a. In the Excel window, on the **PowerPivot** tab, in the **Launch** group, click **PowerPivot Window.**

   b. In the PowerPivot window, on the **Home** tab, in the **Get External Data** group, click **From Text.**

   c. In the **Table Import Wizard,** in the **Connect to Flat File** page, click **Browse.**

   d. In the **Open** dialog box, verify that the C:\084606\Getting Started with PowerPivot folder is selected, select the **Order Details.txt** file, and click **Open.**

---

e. In the **Connect to Flat File** page, from the **Column Separator** drop-down list, select **Tab (t).**

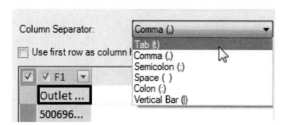

f. Check the **Use first row as column headers** check box, and click **Finish.**

g. In the **Table Import Wizard,** observe the message that the import operation is successful, and click **Close.**

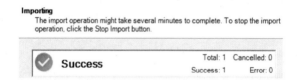

3. Save and close the worksheet.

a. On the Ribbon, select the File tab, and then select **Save As.**

b. In the **Save As** dialog box, in the **File name** text box, type *My Order Details* and click **Save.**

c. Close the My Order Details.xlsx file.

ACTIVITY 1-4
Importing Data from an Excel Worksheet

Data Files:

C:\084606Data\Getting Started With PowerPivot\Stock List.xlsx

Before You Begin:
The Excel application is open.

Scenario:
You have accumulated data pertaining to the inventory of products, and have been analyzing the data using Excel. The market research team in your office has advised you that the stock count will increase substantially because stocks are going to be shipped from a neighboring work place due to renovation work. Analyzing such large amounts of data using Excel would be difficult. Your colleague, who has been using PowerPivot, recommends that you use the same application as it is more efficient with a large data set.

1. Open a new worksheet.

   a. In the Excel window, select the **File** tab, and choose **New.**

   b. In the **Available Templates** section, double-click **Blank workbook.**

2. Select the data to be imported.

   a. In the Excel window, on the **PowerPivot** tab, in the **Launch** group, click **PowerPivot Window.**

   b. In the PowerPivot window, on the **Home** tab, in the **Get External Data** group, click **From Other Sources.**

   c. In the **Table Import Wizard,** in the **Connect to a Data Source** page, scroll down, and in the **Text Files** section, select **Excel File,** and then click **Next.**

   d. In the **Connect to a Microsoft Excel File** page, click **Browse.**

   e. In the **Open** dialog box, verify that the C:\084606Data\Getting Started with PowerPivot folder is selected, select the **Stock List.xlsx** file, and click **Open.**

3. Import the data into the PowerPivot window.

   a. In the **Connect to a Microsoft Excel File** page, check the **Use first row as column headers** check box.

b.   Click **Test Connection,** and in the **PowerPivot for Excel** message box, observe the message that the connection succeeded, click **OK,** and then click **Next.**

c.   In the **Select Tables and Views** page, verify that the **Stock$** check box is checked, and click **Finish.**

d.   In the **Importing** page, click **Close.**

e.   Observe that the data from the Excel worksheet is imported and displayed in the PowerPivot window.

---

4.   Save the workbook.

a.   On the Quick Access toolbar, click the **Save** button.

b.   In the **Save As** dialog box, in the **File name** text box, type *My Stock List*

c.   Click **Save.**

TOPIC C
Refresh Data from a Data Source

You imported data from various data sources. If the source data changes frequently, you may want to keep the imported data up to date. In this topic, you will refresh the imported data.

The data that you import into PowerPivot may be dynamic and subject to constant change, in which case you need to frequently update it. If you are working under tight deadlines, you may not have the time to check for each update, and import the data into a PowerPivot workbook each time. By refreshing the data that is imported, you can rest assured that you are always working with the latest copy of the data.

Data Refresh

Data refresh is the process by which the data that is imported into PowerPivot is replaced by updated data. You can refresh either the data that has been imported in the current worksheet or the data in all the tables of the current PowerPivot workbook.

Connections

A connection is a data link that is established between PowerPivot and a data source. It facilitates the data to be imported into a PowerPivot worksheet. There are three types of connections available: **PowerPivot Data Connections,** which are stored in the PowerPivot workbook, **Local Connections,** which are connections that were previously saved in your document library, and **Workbook Connections**, which are Office Data Connection (.odc) files stored in the PowerPivot workbook. PowerPivot allows you to browse for more connections, open an existing connection, edit a connection, or refresh and delete it.

How to Refresh Data from a Data Source
Procedure Reference: Refresh a Data Set

To refresh a data set:

1. If necessary, import data into a PowerPivot workbook.
2. Refresh data in the workbook.

    *   In the PowerPivot window, on the **Home** tab, in the **Get External Data** group, from the **Refresh** drop-down list, select **Refresh** to refresh data in the current worksheet.
    *   In the **Get External Data** group, from the **Refresh** drop-down list, select **Refresh All** to refresh all the tables in the PowerPivot workbook.
    *   Refresh data for all the tables that use the same connection.

        a. In the PowerPivot window, select the **Design** tab, and in the **Connections** group, click **Existing Connections.**

        b. In the **Existing Connections** dialog box, select a connection, and then click **Refresh.**

Procedure Reference: Change the Filter Settings for an Imported Table

To change the filter settings for an imported table:

1. In the PowerPivot window, select the **Design** tab, and in the **Connections** group, click **Existing Connections.**

2. In the **Existing Connections** dialog box, select the connection for which you want to change filter settings, and click **Open.**

3. In the **Table Import Wizard,** in the **Tables and Views** list box, select a table, and click **Preview & Filter.**

4. In the **Preview Selected Table** page, select the column whose filter settings need to be changed, and then click the drop-down arrow to the right of the column heading.

5. In the AutoFilter menu, check or uncheck check boxes to select filter criteria based on the data in the column and click **OK.**

6. To set advanced filter criteria, click the drop-down list, select **Text Filters** or **Number Filters** and then choose the desired filter criterion. Configure the filter in the **Custom Filter** dialog box and click **OK.**

7. Click **Finish** to import the data with the new filter settings.

Change Filter Settings

After reapplying filters to a table, the values will not be replaced in the existing table, whereas a new worksheet will be created with the filtered values.

Procedure Reference: Modify a Connection

To modify a connection:

1. In the PowerPivot window, select the **Design** tab, and in the **Connections** group, click **Existing Connections.**

2. In the dialog box, select a connection and click **Edit.**

3. In the dialog box, click **Browse** and locate another database of the same type but with a different name.

4. Click **Save** and then click **Close** to close the **Existing Connections** dialog box.

5. On the **Home** tab, in the **Get External Data** group, from the **Refresh** drop-down list, select **Refresh.**

Procedure Reference: Determine the Data Source and Its Last Instance of Refresh

To determine the source of the data:

1. In the PowerPivot window, select the **Design** tab.

2. Determine the desired information.

    ● Determine the data source

        ■ On the **Design** tab, in the **Connections** group, click **Existing Connections.**

        ■ In the **Existing Connections** dialog box, select a data source, and click **Edit.**

        ■ In the **Edit Connection** dialog box, the **Database name** text box provides you with the source of the data.

    ● Determine the last instance of data refresh

        ■ On the **Design** tab, in the **Properties** group, click **Table Properties.**

■ In the **Edit Table Properties** dialog box, in the **Last Refreshed** section, the last instance of data refresh is displayed.

ACTIVITY 1-5
Refreshing Data

Before You Begin:
The My Stock List.xlsx file is open.

Scenario:
You are aware that the stock list that you imported will be subject to frequent change, as products are shipped from the neighboring work place. Because you are working with a very dynamic data set, you decide to refresh the data periodically to ensure that you are working with the updated data set.

---

1. Make changes to the Excel worksheet.

    a. Select the **File** tab and choose **Open**.

    b. In the **Open** dialog box, verify that the C:\084606Data\Getting Started with PowerPivot folder is selected, select the **Stock List.xlsx** file, and click **Open**.

    c. In the Excel window, change the value of cell E2 to **20**

    d. Change the value in cell E3, to **5**

    e. Save the workbook and close it.

---

2. Refresh the data. *My Sbd Liv*

    a. On the **PowerPivot** tab, in the **Launch** group, click **PowerPivot Window**.

    b. Observe that the values in the first and second rows of the Unit Price column are not updated.

Product	Part Number	Vendor	Units On-Hand	Unit Price
Keyboard	286653.24861273	Diamond	1452	$18
Mouse	273719.349052...	Treetop	218	$6
Monitor	224191.706506...	Pile	384	$87
RAM	228201.707229...	Pile	1263	$24

    c. On the **Home** tab, in the **Get External Data** group, click **Refresh.**

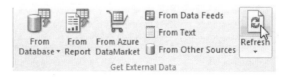

    d. In the **Data Refresh** dialog box, verify that the data refresh is complete, and click **Close.**

---

e. Observe that the values in the first and second rows of the Unit Price column, which were changed in the Excel workbook, are updated.

Product	Part Number	Vendor	Units On-Hand	Unit Price
Keyboard	286653.24861273	Diamond	1452	$20
Mouse	273719.349052...	Treetop	218	$5
Monitor	224191.706506...	Pile	384	$87
RAM	228201.707229...	Pile	1263	$24

3. Determine the last instance of data refresh.

a. Select the **Design** tab, and in the **Properties** group, click **Table Properties.**

b. In the **Edit Table Properties** dialog box, in the **Last Refreshed** section, observe the date and time when the data was last refreshed, and click **Save.**

Clear Row Filters   Last Refreshed: 3/20/2011 7:44:38 PM

              Save   Cancel

c. Save and close the PowerPivot workbook.

ACTIVITY 1-6
Changing the Filter Settings

Before You Begin:

The Excel application is open.

Scenario:

You have received confirmation that the sales data you have is the updated version. You want to import this data along with the data that you have already imported. However, you realize that you need not import all the sales records, but only the information pertaining to select customers.

---

1. Open the existing connection.

   a. Select the **File** tab and choose **Open.**

   b. In the **Open** dialog box, verify that the C:\084606Data\Getting Started with PowerPivot folder is selected.

   c. Select **My Customer Order.xlsx** and click **Open.**

   d. On the **PowerPivot** tab, in the **Launch** group, click **PowerPivot Window.**

   e. Select the **Design** tab, and in the **Connections** group, click **Existing Connections.**

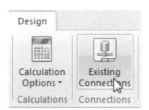

   f. In the **Existing Connections** dialog box, in the **Select an Existing Connection** page, observe that the **Access Customer Order** connection is selected, and click **Open.**

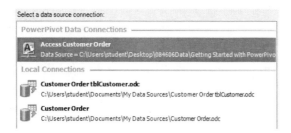

---

2. Change the filter settings for the Sales Invoice worksheet.

   a. In the **Table Import Wizard,** in the **Choose How to Import the Data** page, observe that **Select from a list of tables and views to choose the data to import** option is selected, and click **Next.**

---

b. In the **Select Tables and Views** page, in the **Tables and Views** section, check the **tblSales** check box, and click **Preview & Filter.**

c. In the **Preview Selected Table** page, in the **Table Name: tblSales** section, at the right of the **Customer Name** header, click the drop-down arrow.

d. In the AutoFilter menu, uncheck the **Hexa Web Hosting Services, InfiniTrain,** and **Tri-Mark Properties** check boxes, and click **OK.**

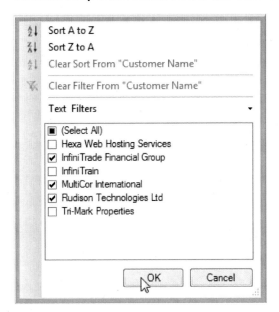

e. In the **Preview Selected Table** page, click **OK.**

f. For the tblSales table, in the **Friendly Name** column, click, and select the existing text and type *Sales Invoice* and then press **Enter.**

g. In the **Table Import Wizard,** click **Finish.**

h. In the **Importing** page, click **Close.**

i. Observe that the invoice details for Rudison Technologies Inc., Multicor International, and InfiniTrade Financial Group are imported.

j. Save and close the workbook.

TOPIC D
Create Linked Tables

You refreshed the data that you imported to ensure that you are working with updated data. Now, you may need to create a table that draws data from an Excel worksheet to reduce data redundancy. In this topic, you will create a linked table.

You may have imported data from an Excel workbook. If the data in the workbook is constantly changing, it will be tedious to update the changes in your PowerPivot workbook. Importing or refreshing the data every time after it is updated can be time consuming. By creating linked tables, you can work with the updated data set without having to refresh the data.

Linked Tables

A linked table is a table created in Excel and linked to a PowerPivot table. A linked table appearing in the PowerPivot window will have the same column names and data as its source table in the Excel worksheet. Any change made to the Excel table will be reflected in the linked PowerPivot table. You can identify a linked table with the chain symbol appearing on the worksheet tab. You can rename, move, or delete a table.

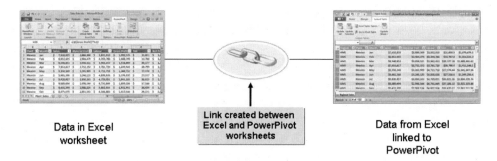

Figure 1-9: *A table in Excel which is linked to a PowerPivot table.*

Automatic Data Refresh

Data in a linked table is automatically refreshed when changes are made to the source data. You can also manually update the data by selecting the **Manual Update** option from the **Refresh** drop-down list.

How to Create Linked Tables

Procedure Reference: Create a Linked Table

To create a linked table:

1. In the Excel window, open a workbook with a table.
2. Select the **PowerPivot** tab, and in the **Excel Data** group, click **Create Linked Table.**
3. If necessary, in the PowerPivot window, rename the worksheet.

    *   In the sheet tab bar, right-click the table name, and select **Rename,** and enter a new name for the table.
    *   In the sheet tab bar, double-click the worksheet tab, type the desired name, and then press **Enter.**

Procedure Reference: Updating Data in Linked Tables

To update data in linked tables:

1. In the PowerPivot window, select the **Linked Table** contextual tab.
2. In the **Linked Tables** group, from the **Update Mode** drop-down list, select an option to set the update mode.

    *   Select **Automatic** to update the data automatically.
    *   Select **Manual** to update the data manually.

Navigate between the Excel and PowerPivot Windows

To navigate from a linked table in the PowerPivot window to the Excel window, select the **Linked Table** contextual tab, and in the **Linked Tables** group, click **Go to Excel Table.**

Making Changes to Linked Table

If you rename a table in Excel after a linked table is created, then the link between the tables is broken. When you attempt to update the data, the **Errors in Linked Tables** dialog box is displayed. In the **Errors in Linked Tables** dialog box, you can click **Options** to select an option and resolve the error.

ACTIVITY 1-7
Creating and Updating Linked Tables

Data Files:

Sales Data.xlsx

Scenario:

You have been provided with a worksheet containing data about the material and labor cost of different manufacturing plants. Because the costs are subject to frequent change depending on their availability, you will be required to change these values constantly. If you import this data into a PowerPivot workbook, you will have to refresh the data every time the source data is modified. You may end up working with outdated data if you forget to refresh the data. You want to avoid the possibility of working with wrong data.

---

1. Open a worksheet to create a linked Excel table.

    a. Select the **File** tab, and choose **Open.**

    b. In the **Open** dialog box, verify that the C:\084606Data\Getting Started with PowerPivot folder is selected, select the **Sales Data.xlsx** file, and click **Open.**

---

2. Create a linked table.

    a. On the **PowerPivot** tab, in the **Excel Data** group, click **Create Linked Table.**

    b. In the **Create Table** dialog box, observe that the cell range A1:I133 is selected and that the **My table has headers** check box is checked, and click **OK.**

    c. Observe that the data is imported into a PowerPivot workbook and a link symbol is displayed besides the worksheet name on the sheet tab bar, indicating that the data from the Excel workbook is linked to the PowerPivot window.

    d. Observe that the **Linked Table** tab is also displayed on the Ribbon.

---

3. Rename the table and update its contents.

---

a.   In the PowerPivot window, in the sheet tab bar, double-click **Table1,** type *Sales Data* and press **Enter.**

b.   On the Quick Access toolbar, click the **Switch to Workbook** button.

c.   Replace the value **$ 2,684,221** in cell E2 with *$ 2685300*

d.   Select the **PowerPivot** tab, and in the **Launch** group, click **PowerPivot Window.**

e.   Observe that the values in the first record reflect the change made in the Excel table.

f.   On the Quick Access toolbar, click the **Switch to Workbook** button.

g.   Save the worksheet as *My Sales Data* and close it.

Lesson 1 Follow-up

In this lesson, you familiarized yourself with the options in the PowerPivot interface and imported data into PowerPivot. Knowing how to use PowerPivot will help you to work effectively with the application and analyze data.

1. **From which data sources are you likely to import data into PowerPivot?**

2. **Which data importing and updating feature in PowerPivot do you think will prove the most useful to you?**

2 | Manipulating PowerPivot Data

Lesson Time: 45 minutes

Lesson Objectives:

In this lesson, you will manipulate data in a PowerPivot worksheet.

You will:

- Organize and format PowerPivot tables.
- Create and manage calculated columns.
- Sort and filter PowerPivot data.
- Create and manage table relationships.

Introduction

You imported data into PowerPivot from various data sources. Once you have the data in place, you may need to break it down and organize it to facilitate easy data analysis. In this lesson, you will manipulate the PowerPivot data.

When you import a large amount of data, the PowerPivot window becomes overloaded. In such cases, data needs to be organized into logical chunks. Knowing various PowerPivot options helps you to manipulate data, gain a better understanding of data trends, eliminate data redundancy, and optimize time.

TOPIC A
Organize and Format Tables

You created a linked table and updated data in it. Now, you need to manipulate data in the table for analysis. In this topic, you will organize and format tables to manipulate data.

The data that you import may consist of a number of columns, each containing data of different types. At times, you may need to display data in a particular format to make it look more professional. For example, you may frequently need to adjust the width of a column to display data completely, or rename a column to provide a better description of data. Knowing how to work with tables will help you to analyze data.

PowerPivot Tables

PowerPivot tables store imported data in a worksheet. Unlike an Excel table, the PowerPivot table does not have any row, column, or cell reference. However, PowerPivot columns have column headers, which can be modified. You cannot type or modify the contents in a PowerPivot table, but you can change the data type of a content. You can paste cells into a new table but not to an existing table. You can also sort data by any column, and filter table data. Tables can be modified by adding or deleting entire columns.

How to Organize and Format Tables

Procedure Reference: Set Table Properties

To set table properties:

1. In the PowerPivot window, select the **Design** tab, and in the **Properties** group, click **Table Properties.**

 The **Table Properties** button is enabled only when the current table contains data imported from an external source. If you copy and paste data from an Excel file or another table, the **Table Properties** button will be disabled.

2. In the **Edit Table Properties** dialog box, set the desired options.

    ● In the **Table Name** text box, enter a new name for the table.

    ● In the **Switch to** section, select the mode in which you want to view the table.

       ■ Select **Table preview** to preview the selected table.

■ Select **Query editor** to view the query that is used to retrieve data from the selected data source.

● In the **Connection Name** text box, enter a connection that will be used to import data.

● In the **Source Name** text box, enter a new source from which the data will be obtained.

● In the **Column Names from** section, select **Source** to replace the current column names with the names from the selected source table, or select **PowerPivot Data** to use the current column names, and ignore the names given in the selected source table.

● Click **Refresh Preview** to view the columns of data in the currently selected source table.

● Click **Clear Row Filters** to remove any filters that are applied to the source data.

3. Click **Save** to apply the changes to the table.

Procedure Reference: Rename a Table

To rename a table:

1. In the PowerPivot window, right-click the worksheet tab and choose **Rename,** or double-click the worksheet tab.

2. Type the desired name for the table and press **Enter.**

Procedure Reference: Move a Table

To move a table:

1. Open the desired PowerPivot workbook.

2. Move a table to the desired location.

● Use the **Move Table** dialog box.

    a. In the PowerPivot window, right-click the worksheet tab and choose **Move.**

    b. In the **Move Table** dialog box, in the **Move selected table before table** list box, select a table before which you want to move the current table.

    c. Click **OK** to move the table to the desired location.

● Click and drag the worksheet tab to the desired location.

Procedure Reference: Delete a Table

To delete a table:

1. In the PowerPivot window, right-click the worksheet tab and choose **Delete.**

2. In the **PowerPivot for Excel** warning box, click **Yes** to delete the table permanently.

Procedure Reference: Manipulate Columns in a Table

To manipulate columns in a table:

1. Open the desired PowerPivot workbook and select a table.

2. Manipulate the columns in the table.

● Add a column.

    a. Select a new column.

      ■ Click the **Add Column** header of the last column in the table.

        ■   Select the **Design** tab, and in the **Columns** group, click **Add.**

   b.   In the Formula Bar, enter a formula and press **Enter.**

●   Rename a column.

        ■   Double-click the column header and type the desired name or;

        ■   Right-click the column, choose **Rename Column** and enter a name for the column.

●   Delete columns.

   a.   Select the columns that you want to delete.

   b.   Delete the selected columns.

        ■   Press **Delete** or;

        ■   In the **Design** tab, in the **Columns** group, click **Delete** or;

        ■   Right-click the column and choose **Delete Columns.**

   c.   In the **PowerPivot for Excel** message box, click **Yes.**

Procedure Reference: Change the Data Type of a Column

To change the data type of a column:

1.   Click a column header to select the column.

2.   On the **Home** tab, in the **Formatting** group, from the **Data Type** drop-down list, select the desired data type.

3.   From the **Format** drop-down list, select the desired data format.

Formatting Values

You cannot apply any additional formatting to a text or boolean data type. You need to select some other data type to apply formatting such as currency, accounting, percentage, and also specify options such as currency format pertaining to a country, thousands separator, and increase or decrease in the decimal places.

Procedure Reference: Hide or Freeze Columns

To hide or freeze columns:

1.   Select the columns to hide or freeze.

2.   Hide or unhide columns in the PowerPivot window.

●   Hide columns using the **Hide and Unhide Columns** dialog box.

   a.   Select the **Design** tab, and in the **Columns** group, click **Hide and Unhide.**

   b.   In the **Hide and Unhide Columns** dialog box, uncheck the check boxes for the columns that you want to hide in the PowerPivot window and those to be excluded from the PivotTable.

   c.   Click **OK** to apply the changes.

●   Right-click the columns which are to be hidden, and then choose **Hide Columns,** and from the submenu choose an option to specify whether it is to be hidden in the PowerPivot table, in a PivotTable, or in both.

●   Unhide columns using the **Hide and Unhide Columns** dialog box.

   a.   Display the **Hide and Unhide Columns** dialog box.

        ■   Select the **Design** tab, and in the **Columns** group, click **Hide and Unhide.**

        ■   Right-click a column and choose **Unhide Columns.**

    b.   In the **Hide and Unhide Columns** dialog box, check the check boxes for the columns that you want to unhide, and then click **OK.**

3.   Freeze or unfreeze a column.

- On the **Home** tab, in the **View** group, click **Freeze** or;

- On the **Home** tab, in the **View** group, click the **Freeze** drop-down arrow, and select **Freeze** or;

- Right-click the column which you want to freeze, and choose **Freeze Columns.**

- Unfreeze a column.

    a.   Select the column which needs to be unfreezed.

    b.   On the **Home** tab, in the **View** group, click **Unfreeze.**

Procedure Reference: Change the Column Widths

To change the column widths:

1.   Select the column whose width is to be changed.

2.   Set the column width.

- Use the **Column Width** dialog box.

    a.   On the **Home** tab, in the **View** group, click **Column Width.**

    b.   In the **Column Width** dialog box, in the **Column width** spin box, set the desired column width.

    c.   Click **OK** to apply the changes.

- Place the mouse pointer at the intersection of two columns and when the mouse pointer changes into a double-headed arrow, click and drag to adjust the width of the column on the left of the mouse pointer.

ACTIVITY 2-1
Managing Table Data

Data Files:

C:\084606Data\Manipulating PowerPivot Data\Customer Order.xlsx, C:\084606Data\
Manipulating PowerPivot Data\Packing Charges.xlsx

Before You Begin:

The Excel 2010 application is open.

Scenario:

You have imported the customer order data into PowerPivot. However, you notice that the data is not final, and additional data is available in an Excel file. You now want to add this data to the PowerPivot workbook and ensure that it is properly organized and formatted.

---

1.   Open the PowerPivot workbook containing the customer order data.

   a.   In the Excel window, select the **File** tab, and choose **Open**.

   b.   In the **Open** dialog box, navigate to the C:\084606Data\Manipulating PowerPivot Data folder.

   c.   Select **Customer Order.xlsx** file and click **Open**.

   d.   On the **PowerPivot** tab, in the **Launch** group, click **PowerPivot Window**.

---

2.   Create a new table from the data in the Packing Charges.xlsx file.

   a.   Switch to Excel, select the **File** tab, and choose **Open**.

   b.   In the **Open** dialog box, verify that the C:\084606\Manipulating PowerPivot Data folder is selected, select **Packing Charges.xlsx** and click **Open**.

   c.   In the Excel worksheet, select the cell range **A1:D7,** and copy the contents.

   d.   Select the **View** tab, and in the **Window** group, from the **Switch Windows** drop-down list, select **Customer Order.xlsx**.

   e.   Select the **PowerPivot** tab, in the **Launch** group, click **PowerPivot Window**.

f.   In the PowerPivot window, on the **Home** tab, in the **Clipboard** group, click **Paste.**

g.   In the **Paste Preview** dialog box, in the **Table Name** text box, type *Special Packing* and click **OK.**

h.   Observe that a table named Special Packing is added to the PowerPivot workbook.

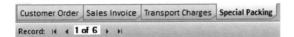

---

3.   Change the data type of the Extra Cost column.

a.   Hover the mouse pointer over the **Extra Cost** column header and when the mouse pointer changes to a downward pointing arrow, click to select the column.

b.   On the **Home** tab, in the **Formatting** group, from the **Data Type: Whole Number** drop-down list, select **Currency.**

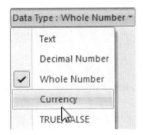

c.   Observe that the values in the Extra Cost column are displayed with a dollar symbol.

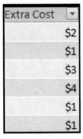

---

4.   Hide the Customer Order column in the PowerPivot window.

a.   Hover the mouse pointer over the **Customer Order** column header, and when the mouse pointer changes to a downward pointing arrow, click to select the column.

b. Select the **Design** tab, and in the **Columns** group, click **Hide and Unhide.**

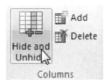

c. In the **Hide and Unhide Columns** dialog box, in the **In PowerPivot window** column, uncheck the **Customer Order** check box.

d. Click **OK** to hide the Customer Order column.

5. Change the width of the Customer Name column.

a. Select the Customer Name column.

b. Select the **Home** tab, and in the **View** group, click **Column Width.**

c. In the **Column Width** dialog box, in the **Column width** text box, double-click and type *200*

d. Click **OK.**

e. Switch to Excel, and select the **View** tab.

f. On the **View** tab, in the **Window** group, from the **Switch Windows** drop-down list, select **Packing Charges.xlsx.**

g. Close the **Packing Charges.xlsx** file.

h. Save the worksheet as *My Customer Order*

TOPIC B

Create Calculated Columns

You renamed, hid, and changed the data type of columns. Now, you may want to create new columns that contain values based on other columns. In this topic, you will create calculated columns.

The data that you import may contain a number of columns, but it may not include all the information you need. For example, you may have information about the rates and quantity of various products sold, but you may need the tax amount as well. You can store the tax amount as a separate column; however, this may cause problems if any of the precedent values such as the rate or quantity sold is updated while the tax amount is not modified. By creating a column that contains values calculated from other columns, you can populate the values automatically for every row and ensure that for any value that is being updated in other columns, the calculated value is also modified accordingly.

Calculated Columns

Definition:

A calculated column is a column that contains automatically populated values, which are based on a formula that is defined for the entire column. Calculated columns are the only columns that can be added to a PowerPivot table. Like any other column, a calculated column can be renamed, deleted, hidden, sorted, or filtered.

Example:

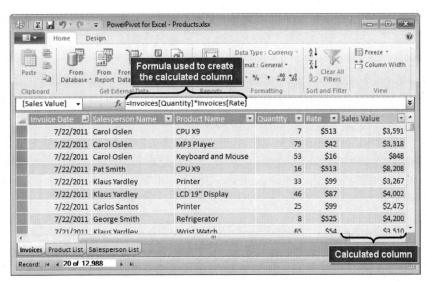

Figure 2-1: A calculated column created using a simple formula.

PowerPivot Formulas

A PowerPivot formula, like an Excel formula, is a symbolic representation that defines a calculation. Formulas always begin with an equal sign (=) and can include references to tables and columns in a PowerPivot workbook. Column names are always enclosed within brackets and are preceded by a table name, though the latter can be omitted if you are referring to a column in the current table. If a table name contains spaces, it must be enclosed within single quotation marks. The AutoComplete feature helps you to type the fully qualified names of columns and tables, and also lists the functions available for use in a formula. When a formula is evaluated, PowerPivot first checks for the general syntax and then checks for the names of columns and tables. If there is any ambiguity with the names, PowerPivot displays an error.

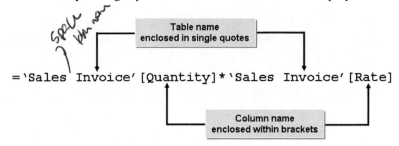

Figure 2-2: *A simple PowerPivot formula used to calculate the sales value.*

How to Create Calculated Columns

Procedure Reference: Create a Calculated Column

To create a calculated column:

1. In the PowerPivot window, select the table for which you want to create a calculated column.
2. Select a new column to use as the calculated column.
    *   Select the **Design** tab, and in the **Columns** group, click **Add** to select a new column in the table.
    *   Click the **Add Column** header of the last column in the table.
3. In the Formula Bar, enter a formula.
4. If necessary, rename the calculated column.
    *   Right-click the column header, choose **Rename Column,** and enter a name for the column or;
    *   Double-click the column header and enter a name for the column.

The AutoComplete Feature

The AutoComplete feature enables you to enter the fully qualified names of tables and columns and also lists the various functions that are available. While creating a calculated column, you can specify the column name in the Formula Bar by selecting the respective columns. You can type the initial few characters of a function, and from the displayed menu in the Formula Bar, you can select the desired function and press **Tab** to include it. You can also enter the arguments for a calculated column by selecting the desired columns.

Procedure Reference: Set the Calculation Options

To set the calculation options:

1. Select a table that has calculated columns.

2. Select the **Design** tab, and in the **Calculation** group, from the **Calculation Options** drop-down list, select an option.

    ● Select **Automatic Calculation Mode** to automatically calculate values in the calculated column.

    ● Select **Manual Calculation Mode** to manually calculate values in the calculated column.

    ● Select **Calculate Now** to recalculate all the values in the table.

Calculate Values Manually

You can also calculate the values manually by pressing the **F9** key.

Procedure Reference: Build a Formula

To build a formula:

1. Click in the Formula Bar.
2. Enter the desired formula, and press **Enter.**

ACTIVITY 2-2
Creating Calculated Columns

Before You Begin:
The My Customer Order.xlsx file is open.

Scenario:
As part of your analysis of customer orders and invoices, you are asked to calculate the tax that would be charged for sales made against orders. You do not want to go back to the source data, add these values, and reimport the data into PowerPivot.

1. Create a calculated column to display the sales value.

   a. In the Excel window, select the **PowerPivot** tab, and in the **Launch** group, click **PowerPivot Window.**

   b. Select the **Sales Invoice** worksheet tab.

   c. In the PowerPivot window, click the **Add Column** column header.

   d. Click on the Formula Bar, and type **=**

   e. Select the **Invoice Quantity** column.

   f. Observe that the column name along with its associated table name is displayed in the Formula Bar.

   > X ✓ *f*x ='Sales Invoice'[Invoice Quantity]

   g. Type ***** and select the **Rate** column, and then press **Enter.**

   h. Scroll to the right, to display the calculated column.

   i. Observe that the column is populated automatically based on the formula that is entered and that the column name is changed to **CalculatedColumn1.**

   j. Double-click the **CalculatedColumn1** column header, type *Sales* and then press **Enter.**

2. Create a calculated column to display the tax levied for the sale.

   a. In the PowerPivot window, click the **Add Column** column header.

   b. Click on the Formula Bar, and type **=**

   c. Select the **Sales** column, type **0.02* and then press **Enter.**

   d. Double-click the **CalculatedColumn1** column header, type *Tax* and then press **Enter.**

   e. On the Quick Access toolbar, click the **Save** button.

TOPIC C

Sort and Filter PowerPivot Data

You created a calculated column. With the data at your disposal, you may realize that you need to arrange it in a specific order and display only selected values. In this topic, you will sort and filter the PowerPivot data to control the data that is used from a table or column.

Not all data that you have in a table may be of use to you. By filtering out unnecessary data, you may have a better picture of the data at your disposal. In tables that involve large volumes of data, you need to arrange it in a logical order.

Sort Options

Sorting data in a PowerPivot table allows you to display it in a specific order. You can sort data based on any column in a table. The sort options vary depending on the data type of a column. Textual data can be sorted in alphabetical or reverse alphabetical order, while numeric data can be sorted in ascending or descending order. Dates can be sorted from oldest to newest or vice versa.

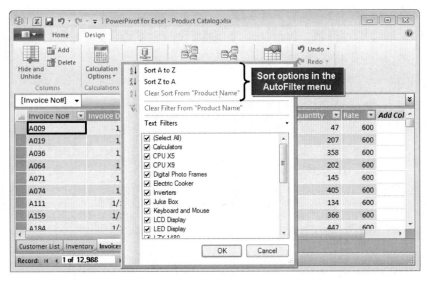

Figure 2-3: Sort options for a text data type column displayed in the AutoFilter menu.

Filter Options

The filtering options in PowerPivot allow you to view rows containing data that meets a specific criteria. Data in a PowerPivot table can be filtered based on a single criterion or multiple criteria. You can filter data using the options in the AutoFilter menu. You can specify a filter condition using one of the default options or setting a custom filter. The default options vary for columns depending on the data type. The AutoFilter menu also allows you to select values for the filter criteria.

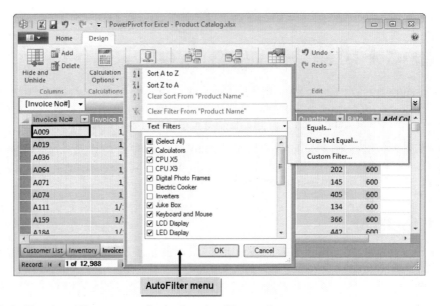

Figure 2-4: *The AutoFilter menu displaying the filter options.*

How to Sort and Filter PowerPivot Data

Procedure Reference: Sort Data

To sort the data:

1. Select the column based on which the PowerPivot table is to be sorted.
2. Sort data.
   - Sort data using the options on the **Home** tab, in the **Sort & Filter** group.
     - Click **Sort Smallest to Largest,** to sort numerical data in the ascending order.
     - Click **Sort Largest to Smallest,** to sort numerical data in descending order.
     - Click **Sort A to Z,** to sort text data in alphabetical order.
     - Click **Sort Z to A,** to sort text data in reverse alphabetical order.
     - Click **Sort Oldest to Newest,** to sort the data ranging from the past to current date entries.
     - Click **Sort Newest to Oldest,** to sort the data ranging from the current entry to the oldest entry.
   - Sort data from the worksheet.
     a. In the column heading of the desired column, click the drop-down arrow.
     b. In the AutoFilter menu, select a sort option.
3. Clear the sort.
   - On the **Home** tab, in the **Sort and Filter** group, click **Clear Sort.**
   - In the column heading of the desired column, click the drop-down arrow, and in the AutoFilter menu, select **Clear Sort From (Column Name).**

Procedure Reference: Filter Data

To filter data:

1. In the column header of the desired column, click the drop-down arrow to display the AutoFilter menu.

2. In the AutoFilter menu, in the list box, select one or more values based on which the table rows will be filtered, and click **OK.**

3. If necessary, customize the filtering options.

   a. In the AutoFilter menu, click the **[Data type] Filters** drop-down arrow, and select an option to display the **Custom Filter** dialog box.

      ● Select **Custom Filter.**

      ● Select a condition based on the data type to display the **Custom Filter** dialog box with the condition set in it.

   b. In the **Custom Filter** dialog box, set the desired filtering criteria, and click **OK.**

4. If necessary, clear a filter.

   ● In the PowerPivot window, on the **Home** tab, in the **Sort and Filter** group, click **Clear All Filters** or;

   ● Right-click a column, and choose **Filter→Clear Filter** or;

   ● Click the drop-down arrow next to the column heading, and in the AutoFilter menu, select **Clear Filter From [Column name].**

ACTIVITY 2-3
Sorting and Filtering Data

Before You Begin:
The My Customer Order.xlsx file is open.

Scenario:
You have been asked to quickly retrieve an important piece of information from the data that you have imported. Your manager has asked for sales details of desktops and laptops arranged in ascending order.

---

1. Filter the PowerPivot data based on product category.

    a. In the Excel window, on the **PowerPivot** tab, in the **Launch** group, click **PowerPivot Window.**

    b. In the **Item Description** column header, click the drop-down arrow.

    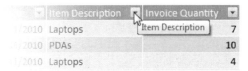

    c. In the displayed AutoFilter menu, uncheck the **PDAs** and **Printers** check boxes, and then click **OK.**

---

2. Sort the PowerPivot data based on sales values.

    a. Select the **Sales** column.

    b. In the column header, click the drop-down arrow, and in the AutoFilter menu, choose **Sort Smallest to Largest.**

    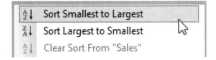

    c. Observe that the values in the **Sales** column are displayed in ascending order.

    d. Save the worksheet.

TOPIC D
Create and Manage Table Relationships

You sorted and filtered data to view the desired data. Now, you may want to reduce data redundancy when it is spread across multiple tables. In this topic, you will create and manage table relationships.

When you have multiple tables at your disposal, you feel that data in a table can be linked with another table to reduce redundancy. For example, if you want to keep track of customer order data, you may notice that separate tables exist for customers, customer discounts, and orders. Updating customer information can turn out to be a tedious and error prone task if the name and contact details of the customer are repeated in all these tables. An alternative way is to include the customer details in a single table, and relate this table to other tables by using a customer identification number or code.

Table Relationships

A table relationship is a connection between two tables based on a column containing common information in each table. The common columns, also called the key columns, usually have the same name in the related tables. A relationship links the key column from one table, which has a unique value in each row, to the key column in the other table, which may or may not have unique values. If you import data from a relational database, and relationships are defined in the source data, then PowerPivot automatically retains the relevant relationships. However, when you import data from a non-relational source such as Excel or text, you may need to create relationships manually.

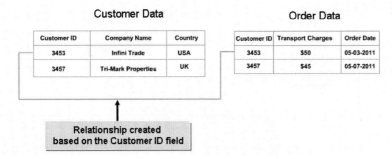

Figure 2-5: A relationship created between two tables based on a common column of data.

Relationship Format

All relationships have the same format: they link a column in a table with a column in another table. Rows in both tables are linked if they share the same values in the key columns.

Types of Relationships

The type of relationship you can create depends on how the columns are related. PowerPivot allows two types of relationships.

Relationship	Description
One-to-Many	Rows in Table A can be matched to any number of rows in Table B. However, a row in Table B can be matched to only one row in Table A.

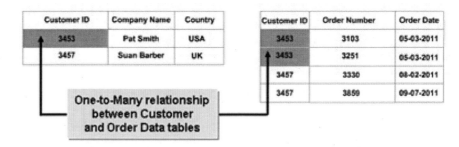

| One-to-One | Rows in Table A can be matched to only one row in Table B and vice versa. The related columns in both tables have unique values. |

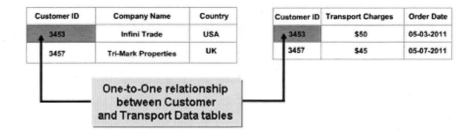

The Create Relationship Dialog Box

The **Create Relationship** dialog box is used to create a relationship between tables in a PowerPivot workbook. You must select a table for which you need to create a relationship and a source column, which will be used to establish the relationship. You must also select a related lookup table and a column in the table, which is related to the column in the first table. Every row in the **Related LookUp Column** must have a unique value.

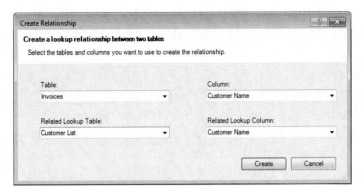

Figure 2-6: *The Create Relationship dialog box displaying options to establish a relationship between two tables.*

The Manage Relationships Dialog Box

The **Manage Relationships** dialog box provides you with options to create a new relationship, edit existing relationships, and delete relationships. It lists the existing relationships in a workbook. You can sort the order in which these relationships are displayed, either by table or lookup table.

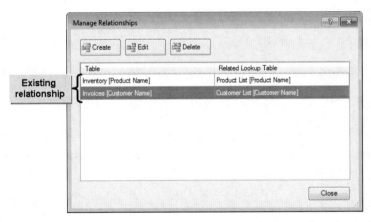

Figure 2-7: *The Manage Relationships dialog box displaying a list of existing relationships.*

How to Create and Manage Table Relationships

Procedure Reference: Create a Relationship

To create a relationship:

1. In the PowerPivot window, select the **Design** tab, and in the **Relationships** group, click **Create Relationship.**

2. In the **Create Relationship** dialog box, from the **Table** drop-down list, select a table for which you need to establish a relationship.

3. From the **Column** drop-down list, select a column that contains data to be related.

4. From the **Related Lookup Table** drop-down list, select a table that has a key column, which is related to the table selected in the **Table** section.

5. From the **Related Lookup Column** drop-down list, select a key column, which has distinct values, and matches with the column selected in the **Column** section.

6. Click **Create** to create a table relationship.

Conditions to Create a Table Relationship

To create a relationship between two tables, you need to adhere to certain conditions:

- You can create only one relationship between a pair of tables.

- The column selected in the **Related Lookup Column** section must have unique values, without any duplicates.

- The data types of the columns selected in the **Column** and **Related Lookup Column** sections must be compatible with each other.

Procedure Reference: Edit Relationships

To edit the relationships:

1. In the PowerPivot window, select the **Design** tab, and in the **Relationships** group, click **Manage Relationships.**

2. In the **Manage Relationships** dialog box, in the list box, select the relationship that you want to edit, and click **Edit.**

3. In the **Edit Relationship** dialog box, using the **Table, Column, Related Lookup Table,** and **Related Lookup Column** text boxes, edit the relationship according to your needs, and then click **OK.**

4. In the **Manage Relationships** dialog box, click **Close.**

ACTIVITY 2-4
Creating and Managing Relationships

Before You Begin:
The My Customer Order.xlsx file is open.

Scenario:
You are asked to compute additional transportation costs incurred by the company for orders placed to date. However, you realize that the transportation costs are maintained according to invoice number. Thus, you need to first identify invoice details for every order and then calculate the transportation costs for the identified invoices.

---

1. Create a relationship to identify the invoices for a customer order.

    a. In the Excel window, on the **PowerPivot** tab, in the **Launch** group, click **PowerPivot Window.**

    b. Select the **Design** tab, and in the **Relationships** group, click **Create Relationship.**

    c. In the **Create Relationship** dialog box, in the **Table** drop-down list, verify that **Sales Invoice** is selected.

    d. From the **Column** drop-down list, select **Customer Order.**

    e. From the **Related Lookup Table** drop-down list, select **Customer Order.**

    f. In the **Related Lookup Column** drop-down list, verify that **Customer Order** is selected, and click **Create** to create the relationship.

---

2. Create a relationship to identify the transportation cost associated with each invoice.

    a. On the **Design** tab, in the **Relationships** group, click **Create Relationship.**

    b. In the **Create Relationship** dialog box, in the **Table** drop-down list, verify that **Sales Invoice** is selected.

    c. From the **Column** drop-down list, select **Invoice Number.**

    d. From the **Related Lookup Table** drop-down list, select **Transport Charges.**

e.   In the **Related Lookup Column** drop-down list, verify that **Invoice Number** is selected and click **Create** to create the relationship.

3.   View the relationships that were created.

a.   On the **Design** tab, in the **Relationships** group, click **Manage Relationships.**

b.   In the **Manage Relationships** dialog box, in the list box, observe the relationships listing their tables and related lookup tables, and then click **Close.**

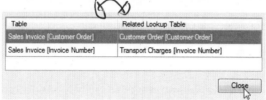

1 : many

c.   Save and close the workbook.

Left onto

Lesson 2 Follow-up

In this lesson, you manipulated data in a PowerPivot worksheet. By manipulating data, you can reduce data redundancy and display only select sets of data that are of interest to you. This will improve your data analysis and optimize your time.

1. **Which data manipulation techniques do you frequently use during the course of your work?**

2. **Give some examples of calculated columns that you would add in PowerPivot.**

3 | Creating PowerPivot Reports

Lesson Time: 1 hour(s), 15 minutes

Lesson Objectives:

In this lesson, you will create reports using PowerPivot data.

You will:

- Create a PivotTable to present data in a tabular form.
- Create PivotCharts to represent data in a graphical manner.
- Use slicers to filter the desired data.
- Present PivotTable data visually.

Introduction

You manipulated data in PowerPivot, thereby preparing data for analysis. You may want to generate reports to present and analyze data in an effective manner. In this lesson, you will create reports from PowerPivot data.

Going through rows of data to extract specific information can be tedious. Sometimes, you may want to analyze a specific set of data and compare it with another set of data. With the help of PowerPivot reporting tools, you can create interactive reports to compare and analyze large amounts of data with ease.

TOPIC A
Create a PivotTable

You stored a large amount of data in PowerPivot for analysis. Analyzing such data becomes tedious; however, this could be made easier by summarizing data and extracting the required information. In this topic, you will create a PivotTable to analyze data.

Analyzing data from large tables is a cumbersome and time consuming task. Moreover, you may not be able to perform a detailed data analysis. You need to extract specific information by summarizing and forecasting values that are not apparent. By using PivotTables, you can quickly summarize and categorize large data sets to perform a detailed analysis.

PivotTables

A *PivotTable* is an interactive worksheet table used to quickly summarize and analyze large amounts of spreadsheet data. It displays data in a matrix format and provides specialized functionality that enables you to summarize and group selected portions of the data to see new data relationships. You can also pivot data between columns and rows to create a concise and customized output. To specify the source data used in a PivotTable report, you need to first identify the required fields and items. Fields are categories of data, usually columns, and items are subcategories in a field.

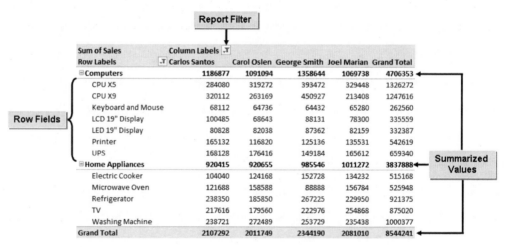

Figure 3-1: A PivotTable displaying sales made by different salespersons under two different product categories.

Flattened PivotTables

A *flattened PivotTable* is a PivotTable, which is used to display data in groups. Every column has a heading under which data can be grouped. Instead of arranging some data values as column headers and others as row headers, a new column is added for each field that you add, and a Totals row is added after each group.

Salesperson Name	Product Name	Product Category	Sum of Sales
Andrea Pitson	Calculator	Miscellaneous	96192
Andrea Pitson	Calculator Total		96192
Andrea Pitson Total			96192
Bobby Thomas	Calculator	Miscellaneous	87228
Bobby Thomas	Calculator Total		87228
Bobby Thomas Total			87228

Fields appearing as columns

Figure 3-2: A flattened PivotTable displaying sales made by various salesperson under four different product categories grouped into columns.

The PowerPivot Field List Pane

The **PowerPivot Field List** pane is displayed when you create a PivotTable from PowerPivot data. It provides you with options to manipulate a PivotTable interactively. This pane includes drop zones, where you can place fields to quickly rearrange data and calculated values in different formats. The **Report Filter** drop zone is used to specify fields that you want to use to filter data in a PivotTable report. The **Row Labels** and **Column Labels** drop zones are used to specify information that is to be displayed in rows and columns respectively. The **Values** drop zone is used to specify values that are to be displayed in the cells of a PivotTable. The **Slicers Vertical** and **Slicers Horizontal** drop zones are used to display slicers, which allow you to filter data in a PivotTable.

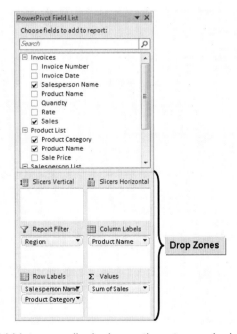

Figure 3-3: The PowerPivot Field List pane displaying options to manipulate a PivotTable.

Differences Between the PivotTable Field List Pane and the PowerPivot Field List Pane

When PivotTables created in Excel are selected, the **PivotTable Field List** pane is displayed. This pane slightly differs from the **PowerPivot Field List** pane that is displayed when you select a PivotTable created from PowerPivot. The **Slicers Vertical** and **Slicers Horizontal** drop zones are displayed only in the **PowerPivot Field List** pane. The **PivotTable Field List** pane on the other hand contains the **Defer Layout Update** check box, which allows you to prevent any change from happening to the layout of a PivotTable when fields are being manipulated in the pane. Once you make changes and click **Update,** all changes come into effect.

How to Create a PivotTable

Procedure Reference: Create a PivotTable

To create reports using PivotTable:

1. In the PowerPivot window, on the **Home** tab, in the **Reports** group, click **PivotTable.**
2. In the **Create PivotTable** dialog box, specify the location for the PivotTable.
    *   Select the **New Worksheet** option to place the PivotTable in a new worksheet.
    *   Select the **Existing Worksheet** option and in the **Location** text box, specify the cell reference to place the PivotTable.
3. Click **OK** to close the **Create PivotTable** dialog box.
4. In the **PowerPivot Field List** pane, select the layout of the fields.
    *   In the **Choose fields to add to report** list box, select the respective fields by checking the check boxes.
    *   Drag the fields that contain numerical values to the **Values** drop zone.
    *   Drag the desired fields to the **Column Labels** or **Row Labels** drop zone.
    *   Drag the fields by which you want to filter the report to the **Report Filter** drop zone.
    *   Right-click a field in any drop zone and choose an option to move the field to another drop zone.
    *   Right-click a field in any drop zone and choose **Remove Field** to remove the field from the PivotTable.

Procedure Reference: Create a Flattened PivotTable

To flatten the PivotTable for simplifying the report.

1. In the PowerPivot window, on the **Home** tab, in the **Report** group, click the **PivotTable** drop-down arrow, and from the displayed list, select **Flattened PivotTable.**
2. In the **Create Flattened PivotTable** dialog box, specify the location for the PivotTable.
    *   Select a **New Worksheet** option to place the flattened PivotTable in a new worksheet.
    *   Select the **Existing Worksheet** option and in the **Location** text box, specify the cell reference to place the flattened PivotTable.
3. In the **PowerPivot Field List** pane, select fields and define the layout of the PivotTable.

Procedure Reference: Delete a PivotTable

To delete a PivotTable.

1. Select the PivotTable to be deleted.
2. On the keyboard, press **Delete.**

ACTIVITY 3-1
Creating a PivotTable

Data Files:

Products.xlsx

Before You Begin:

The Excel 2010 application is open.

Scenario:

You have a large amount of data on product sales in different regions for four years. Your manager has asked you to present a report based on the products sold by each salesperson in different regions. He also wants you to provide the means to compare the performances of the sales persons.

---

1. Insert a blank PivotTable from PowerPivot data.

    a. In the Excel window, select the **File** tab, and choose **Open**.

    b. In the **Open** dialog box, navigate to the C:\084606Data\Creating PowerPivot Reports folder.

    c. Open the **Products.xlsx** file.

    d. Launch the PowerPivot window.

    e. In the PowerPivot window, on the **Home** tab, in the **Reports** group, click **PivotTable.**

    f. In the **Create PivotTable** dialog box, select the **Existing Worksheet** option and in the **Location** text box, verify that cell A1 in Sheet1 is specified, and click **OK.**

g.   Observe that a blank PivotTable is displayed in the Excel worksheet.

2.   Insert fields in the PivotTable to display the product-wise sales made by each salesperson.

a.   In the **PowerPivot Field List** pane, in the **Choose fields to add to report** list box, in the **Invoices** section, check the **Salesperson Name** and **Sales** check boxes.

b.   Observe that the Salesperson Name field is added to the **Row Labels** drop zone, and the Sum of Sales field is added to the **Values** drop zone.

c.   In the **Choose fields to add to report** list box, expand the **Product List** section.

d.   In the **Product List** section, check the **Product Category** and **Product Name** check boxes.

e.   Observe that the Product Category and Product Name fields are added to the **Row Labels** drop zone.

f.   In the **Choose fields to add to report** list box, scroll down and expand the **Salesperson List** section, and then check the **Region** check box.

g.   In the **PowerPivot Field List** pane, from the **Row Labels** drop zone, drag the **Region** field to the **Report Filter** drop zone.

h. From the **Row Labels** drop zone, drag the **Salesperson Name** field to the **Column Labels** drop zone.

i. Observe that the PivotTable displays data based on the fields added to the different drop zones.

3. Compare the sales made by Carlos Santos and Joel Marian.

a. In the Excel worksheet, click the **Column Labels** drop-down arrow, and in the AutoFilter menu, uncheck the **(Select All)** check box.

b. Check the **Carlos Santos** and **Joel Marian** check boxes, and click **OK**.

c. Observe that sales made by the selected salespersons are displayed in the Pivot-Table for comparison.

d. In the Excel window on the sheet tab bar, right-click **Sheet1** and choose **Rename**.

e. Type *Sales Report* and press **Enter** to rename the worksheet.

f. Save the workbook as *My Products*

ACTIVITY 3-2
Creating a Flattened PivotTable

Before You Begin:

The My Products.xlsx file is open.

Scenario:

You have another request from your manager for additional data. He wants a report that will allow him to analyze the category-wise performance of each salesperson. You want to present the information as a simple table that can be manipulated to derive the required results.

---

1. Insert a blank flattened PivotTable.

    a. In the Excel worksheet, on the sheet tab bar, select **Sheet2.**

    b. Launch the PowerPivot window.

    c. On the **Home** tab, in the **Reports** group, click the **PivotTable** drop-down arrow, and from the displayed list, select **Flattened PivotTable.**

    d. In the **Create Flattened PivotTable** dialog box, select the **Existing Worksheet** option, and in the **Location** text box, verify that cell A1 in Sheet2 is specified, and click **OK.**

---

2. Select the fields to be inserted in the flattened PivotTable to analyze sales by various salespersons.

    a. In the **PowerPivot Field List** pane, in the **Choose fields to add to report** list box, in the **Invoices** section, check the **Salesperson Name** and **Sales** check boxes.

    b. Expand the **Product List** section and check the **Product Category** check box.

    c. From the **Row Labels** drop zone, drag the **Product Category** field into the **Column Labels** drop zone.

    d. Observe that the flattened PivotTable is displayed in the Excel worksheet.

    e. Rename the worksheet as *Product Sales*

---

3. Analyze the sales of computers.

    a. In the Excel worksheet, in the PivotTable, click the **Product Category** drop-down arrow, and in the AutoFilter menu, uncheck the **(Select All)** check box.

    b. Check the **Computers** check box and then click **OK.**

    c. Observe that only the total sales value of products in the Computers category is displayed for each salesperson.

    d. Save the workbook.

TOPIC B
Create PivotCharts

You created PivotTable reports. Another way of generating a report is to create a PivotChart to represent data graphically. In this topic, you will create PivotCharts.

Graphical representation of data makes analysis easier. Though PivotTables generate reports that are easy to understand, you may want to show a visual representation of data; for example, in cases where there is a trend over time, such as growth or decline on a monthly or yearly basis. In this case, you may want to focus on a particular quarter to highlight revenue growth. PivotChart reports facilitate data analysis by graphically representing data.

PivotCharts

A *PivotChart* is an interactive chart that graphically represents data in a PivotTable report. When you create a PivotChart report, a PivotTable report associated with the chart is also created. A PivotChart contains standard chart elements and allows you to make modifications such as changing the chart type or layout. Unlike a regular chart, a PivotChart is tied to its Pivot-Table report for data and not to worksheet cells. A PivotChart, therefore, represents only the current state of the PivotTable report. PivotCharts also provide options to filter data by using the drop-down lists displayed on them.

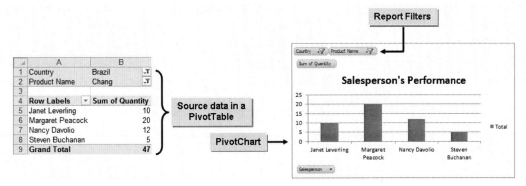

Figure 3-4: A PivotChart visually representing the data from a PivotTable.

PivotChart Types

You can create reports from PowerPivot by using different types of PivotCharts.

Type	Description
PivotChart	Create a blank PivotChart on a new worksheet or a worksheet of your choice.

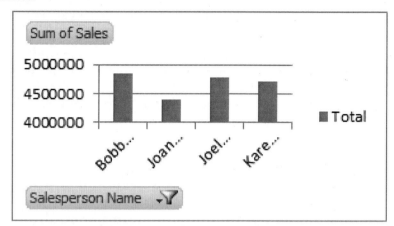

Chart and Table Horizontal	Create a blank PivotChart and PivotTable on a new worksheet or a worksheet of your choice, and place them side-by-side. You can change their positions.

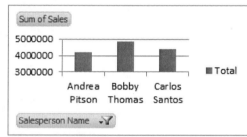

Row Labels	Sum of Sales
Andrea Pitson	4199592
Bobby Thomas	4857318
Carlos Santos	4421230
Grand Total	**13478140**

Type	Description
Chart and Table Vertical	Create a blank PivotChart and PivotTable on a new worksheet or a worksheet of your choice, and place them with the chart above the table. You can change their positions.

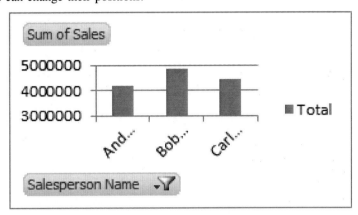

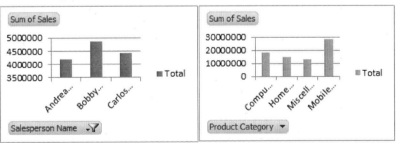

Two Charts Horizontal	Create two blank PivotCharts on a new worksheet or a worksheet of your choice, and place them side-by-side.

Type	Description
Two Charts Vertical	Create two blank PivotCharts on a new worksheet or a worksheet of your choice, and place them one above the other.

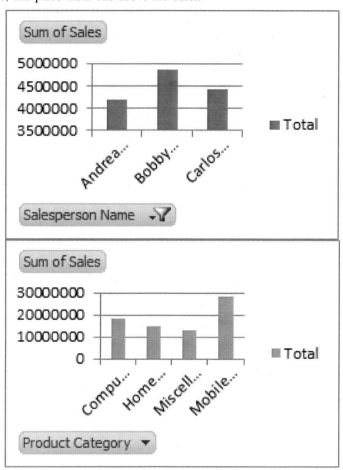

Four Charts	Create four blank PivotCharts on a new worksheet or a worksheet of your choice. The charts are independent of each other.

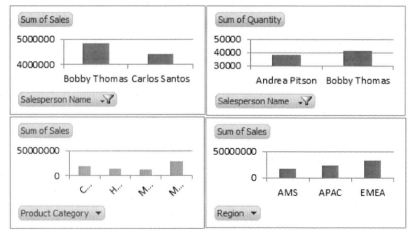

How to Create PivotCharts

Procedure Reference: Create a PivotChart

To insert a PivotChart:

1. In the PowerPivot window, on the **Home** tab, in the **Reports** group, from the **PivotTable** drop-down list, select an option to insert a PivotChart on a worksheet.

2. In the **Create PivotChart** dialog box, specify the location for the PivotChart.

   - Select the **New Worksheet** option to insert a PivotChart in a new worksheet.

   - Select the **Existing Worksheet** option, and specify the worksheet and cell reference to insert a PivotChart in an existing worksheet in the desired location.

3. Click **OK** to insert the PivotChart.

4. Use the **PowerPivot Field List** pane to construct the PivotChart by adding fields to the drop zones. The PivotTable and PivotChart will then appear in their respective worksheets.

Delete a PivotChart

To delete a PivotChart, select it and on the keyboard, press **Delete.**

ACTIVITY 3-3
Creating a PivotChart

Before You Begin
The My Products.xlsx file is opened.

Scenario:
You have been asked to provide a report to review and compare sales of different products by various salespersons in different regions. Working with data in tabular form may be cumbersome. So you decide to represent data in a graphical manner that will be easier to interpret.

---

1. Create a blank PivotChart.

    a. In the Excel window, select **Sheet3.**

    b. Launch the PowerPivot window.

    c. In the PowerPivot window, on the **Home** tab, in the **Reports** group, click the **Pivot-Table** drop-down arrow, and from the displayed list, select **Two Charts (Horizontal).**

    d. In the **Create Two PivotCharts (Horizontal)** dialog box, select the **Existing Worksheet** option, and in the **Location** text box, verify that cell A1 in Sheet3 is specified, and click **OK.**

    e. Observe that two blank PivotCharts are inserted in the worksheet.

---

2. Insert fields into the first PivotChart to compare category-wise sales for salespersons.

    a. Select **Chart 1.**

    b. In the **PowerPivot Field List** pane, in the **Choose fields to add to report** list box, in the **Invoices** section, check the **Sales** and **Salesperson Name** check boxes.

    c. Expand the **Product List** section and check the **Product Category** check box.

    d. In the **Axis Fields** drop zone, drag the **Salesperson Name** field and place it below the **Product Category** field.

    e. Observe that the PivotChart is generated in the Excel worksheet.

---

3. Remove PivotChart elements.

    a. On the worksheet, select the first chart.

    b. Select the **PivotChart Tools Layout** contextual tab, and in the **Labels** group, from the **Chart Title** drop-down list, select **None.**

---

    c.   From the **Legend** drop-down list, select **None.**

4.   Analyze sales of different product categories and salespersons.

    a.   In the PivotChart, click the **Product Category** filter drop-down arrow, and in the AutoFilter menu, uncheck the **(Select All)** check box.

    b.   Check the **Home Appliances** check box and click **OK.**

    c.   Observe that the PivotChart displays the sales graph for all salespersons for the Home Appliances product category.

    d.   In the PivotChart, click the **Salesperson Name** filter drop-down arrow, and in the AutoFilter menu, uncheck the **(Select All)** check box.

    e.   Check the **Carol Oslen** and **Karen Frank** check boxes and click **OK.**

    f.   Click the **Product Category** filter drop-down arrow, and in the AutoFilter menu, check the **(Select All)** check box and click **OK.**

    g.   Observe that the PivotChart displays the sales graph for the selected salespersons for all product categories.

5.   Insert fields into the second PivotChart to compare the region-wise product sales.

    a.   Scroll to the right and select **Chart 2.**

    b.   In the **PowerPivot Field List** pane, in the **Choose fields to add to report** list box, in the **Invoices** section, check the **Quantity** check box.

    c.   Expand the **Product List** section and check the **Product Name** check box. Scroll down, expand the **Salesperson List** section, and check the **Region** check box.

    d.   From the **Axis Fields** drop zone, drag the **Region** field to the **Legend Fields** drop zone.

    e.   Observe that the second PivotChart displays the region-wise sales.

6.   Analyze the mobile phone product sales in various regions.

    a.   In the PivotChart, click the **Product Name** filter drop-down arrow, and in the AutoFilter menu, uncheck the **(Select All)** check box.

    b.   Check the **CDMA, CDMA2000** and **GSM** check boxes. Scroll down, check the **WCDMA** check box and click **OK.**

    c.   Observe that the PivotChart displays the sales graph for different mobile phone products for all regions.

    d.   In the PivotChart, click the **Region** filter drop-down arrow, and in the AutoFilter menu, uncheck the **(Select All)** check box.

    e.   Check the **AMS** check box and click **OK.** Observe that the PivotChart displays the sales graph for different mobile phone products for the AMS region alone.

    f.   Rename the worksheet as *Sales Chart* and save the workbook.

TOPIC C
Filter Data Using Slicers

You created PivotTables and PivotCharts to analyze data. At times, they are overloaded with information and you need an easy mechanism to manipulate only specific data and view it. In this topic, you will filter data in PivotTables and PivotCharts using slicers.

Though you can filter data in a PivotTable using filters and by using the drop zones in the **PowerPivot Field List** pane; it may not be easy to understand what data you are looking for, when multiple filters have been applied. A simple filtering mechanism is essential to filter data, as well as quickly understand the current state of a PivotTable or PivotChart, and also to analyze data easily. Excel provides slicers to filter data with ease.

Slicers

A slicer is a filtering tool that provides you with options to include only the required elements in a PivotTable or PivotChart. Using slicers, you can add and remove elements from a Pivot-Table or PivotChart so that the data can be compared and evaluated from different perspectives. Excel allows you to create more than one slicer for a PivotTable or PivotChart. You can also use the same slicer with multiple PivotTables to showcase data consistently in a variety of scenarios. Slicers can be placed either on the same worksheet that contains the PivotTable or on a different worksheet.

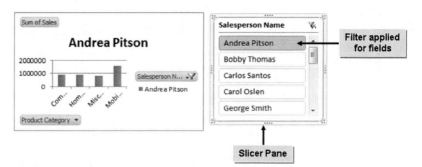

Figure 3-5: A PivotChart displaying data based on a field selected in a slicer.

How to Filter Data Using Slicers

Procedure Reference: Apply Slicers to a PivotTable or PivotChart

To apply slicers to a PivotTable or PivotChart:

1. Insert a PivotTable or PivotChart.

2. Display the **Insert Slicers** dialog box.

    *   Select the PivotChart or PivotTable and in the Excel window, select the **Insert** tab, and in the **Filter** group, click **Slicer.**

    *   Select the PivotTable and in the **PivotTable Tools Options** contextual tab, in the **Sort & Filter** group, click **Insert Slicer.**

    *   Select the PivotChart and in the **PivotChart Tools Analyze** contextual tab, in the **Data** group, click **Insert Slicer.**

3. In the **Insert Slicers** dialog box, check the check boxes for fields which you want to display slicers.

4. Click **OK** to close the **Insert Slicers** dialog box.

5. Apply a filter using a slicer.

    *   In a slicer, select a field, to filter values by the field in a PivotTable or PivotChart.

    *   Hold down **Ctrl** and click additional fields to filter the PivotTable or PivotChart by multiple fields values.

    *   Hold down **Shift** and click a field to filter the PivotTable or PivotChart by a set of consecutive field values.

ACTIVITY 3-4
Filtering Data Using Slicers

Before You Begin:

The My Product.xlsx file is open.

Scenario:

You have been asked to provide a few charts to highlight sales of different products by sales-persons. George Smith, Joseph Matsuda, and Susan Yong have been identified as the salespersons who have notched up highest sale of computers. You need to provide a chart comparing their sales of specific products. You have inserted PivotCharts to display the salesperson names and the products sold by them in different regions. At times, the PivotChart may contain too much information or you may want to display only selected fields in the PivotChart, so you decide to use the slicers feature, to isolate the products, and help you analyze them in detail.

---

1. Modify the PivotChart and display slicers.

   a. In the Sales Chart worksheet, verify that the second chart is selected.

   b. In the **PowerPivot Field List** pane, scroll up and in the **Choose fields to add to report** list box, in the **Invoices** section, check the **Salesperson Name** check box.

   c. Select the **PivotChart Tools Analyze** contextual tab, and in the **Show/Hide** group, click **Field Buttons** to hide the filter fields in the chart.

   d. In the **Data** group, click **Insert Slicer.**

   e. In the **Insert Slicers** dialog box, in the **Invoices** section, check the **Salesperson Name** check box.

   f. In the **Product List** section, check the **Product Name** check box.

   g. Scroll down, and in the **Salesperson List** section, check the **Region** check box, and click **OK.**

   h. In the Excel worksheet, scroll to the left.

   i. Rearrange the slicer panes on the worksheet.

---

2. Apply slicers to compare sales of CPU X5 and CPU X9 by the top three salespersons.

   a. In the **Region** slicer, on the top right corner, click the **Clear Filter** button.

   b. In the **Product Name** slicer, select **CPU X5.**

   c. Hold down **Ctrl** and select **CPU X9.**

   d. In the **Salesperson Name** slicer, select **George Smith.**

   e. Hold down **Ctrl** and select **Joseph Matsuda** and **Susan Yong.**

---

3. Filter data to display sales of CPU X9 by all salesperson in all the regions.

---

a.   In the **Salesperson Name** slicer, click the **Clear Filter** button.

b.   In the **Product Name** slicer pane, select **CPU X9.**

c.   Save the workbook.

TOPIC D
Present PivotTable Data Visually

You created reports using PivotTables and PivotCharts and you filtered data using slicers. Now, you may want to add rich visual representation of data to your reports. In this topic, you will present PivotTable data visually.

Charts are an ideal way of representing data visually. Sometimes, they occupy more space on a worksheet and may even obstruct data. You may want to represent data visually without blocking too much space. In such cases, sparklines serve as an effective tool to create small charts within a cell.

Sparklines

Definition:

A sparkline is a tiny chart that is embedded in a cell to represent the trend for a given range, which can be a row or column. Unlike a chart, a sparkline can be used as a cell background. Moreover, you can create a sparkline for a single range and then extend it to multiple ranges using the fill handle.

Example:

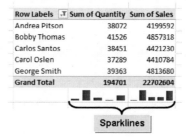

Figure 3-6: Sparklines displaying the trends in values in each column.

Types of Sparklines

There are three types of sparklines you can use in Excel.

Sparkline Type	Description
Line	Data trends are displayed in the form of a straight or zigzag line.

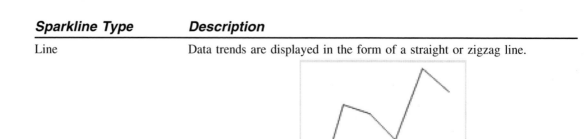

Sparkline Type	Description
Column	Data trends are displayed in the form of columns. Each data value is represented by a column whose size is proportional to the data value.

| Win\Loss | Data trends are displayed through the high, median, and low points. |

Markers

Markers are used to highlight a point where the orientation of the trendline changes. Markers can be applied only to line sparklines.

The Sparkline Tools Design Contextual Tab

The **Sparkline Tools Design** contextual tab helps you to customize sparklines when a cell or range containing sparklines is selected. This tab includes five groups with formatting options for sparklines.

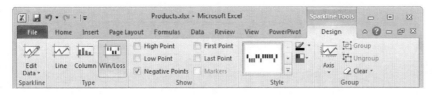

Figure 3-7: The Sparkline Tools Design contextual tab displaying options to edit sparklines.

Group	Description
Sparkline	Contains options for editing the source data of sparklines and modifying the location of a sparkline.
Type	Allows you to choose any of the three types of sparklines: line, column, and win\loss.

Group	Description
Show	Contains check boxes for displaying or hiding high points, low points, negative points, first point, last point, and markers. The **Marker** check box is disabled for column and win\loss type sparklines.
Style	Contains the styles gallery for sparklines. Also contains drop-down arrows that launch galleries for sparkline and marker colors.
Group	Contains options for grouping or ungrouping sparklines so that they can share similar formatting. Grouping sparklines is similar to the grouping of graphical objects. Any formatting applied to a sparkline will be automatically applied to other sparklines of the group.

Conditional Formatting

Definition:

Conditional formatting is a technique that applies a specified format to a selected cell or range of cells in a PivotTable based upon a set of predefined criteria. In a PivotTable, the cells to be formatted can contain numeric or textual data. The condition for formatting can be set using default or user defined rules. If the conditions that you specified are met, then the formatting is applied. You can control the cell font, fill color, and apply a border setting based on the selected cell's contents or based on the contents of another cell.

Example:

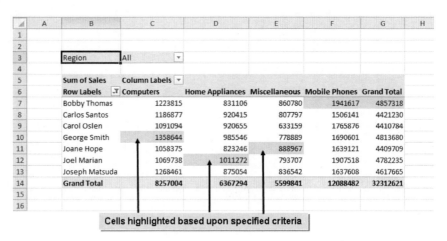

Figure 3-8: *Conditional formatting applied to highlight the highest value in each category.*

Conditional Formats

Excel provides different types of conditional formats that can be applied using the **Conditional Formatting** option in the **Styles** group on the **Home** tab.

Format	*Used to*
Highlight Cell Rules	Find specific cells within a range of cells. You can format those cells based on a comparison operator. This format is applied by selecting the desired option displayed in the **Highlight Cell Rules** submenu.

Row Labels .T	Sum of Sales
Andrea Pitson	4199592
Bobby Thomas	4857318
Carlos Santos	4421230
Carol Oslen	4410784
George Smith	4813680
Joane Hope	4409709
Grand Total	**27112313**

Format	*Used to*
Top/Bottom Rules	Find the highest and lowest values in a range of cells based on a cutoff value you specify. This format is applied by selecting the desired option in the **Top/Bottom Rules** submenu.

Row Labels .T	Sum of Sales
Andrea Pitson	4199592
Bobby Thomas	4857318
Carlos Santos	4421230
Carol Oslen	4410784
George Smith	4813680
Joane Hope	4409709
Grand Total	**27112313**

Format	Used to
Data Bars	View the value of a cell relative to other cells. The length of a data bar represents the value in a cell. This format is applied by selecting a data bar format from the **Data Bars** gallery. A data bar can be customized if required.

Row Labels	Sum of Sales
Andrea Pitson	4199592
Bobby Thomas	4857318
Carlos Santos	4421230
Carol Oslen	4410784
George Smith	4813680
Joane Hope	4409709
Grand Total	**27112313**

Format	Used to
Color Scales	Represent data distribution and variation visually. The shade of the color in this format represents higher, middle or lower values. This format is applied by selecting a color scale format from the **Color Scales** gallery. A color scale can be customized, if required.

Row Labels	Sum of Sales
Andrea Pitson	4199592
Bobby Thomas	4857318
Carlos Santos	4421230
Carol Oslen	4410784
George Smith	4813680
Joane Hope	4409709
Grand Total	**27112313**

Format	Used to
Icon Sets	Annotate and classify data into three or five categories. Each category is represented by an icon. This format is applied by selecting an icon set type from **Icon Sets** gallery. An icon set can be customized if required.

Row Labels	Sum of Sales
Andrea Pitson ⬇	4199592
Bobby Thomas ⬆	4857318
Carlos Santos ↘	4421230
Carol Oslen ↘	4410784
George Smith ⬆	4813680
Joane Hope ↘	4409709
Grand Total	**27112313**

The Conditional Formatting Rules Manager Dialog Box

The **Conditional Formatting Rules Manager** dialog box is used to define one or more conditional format rules. This dialog box can be used to create, edit, and delete a rule. It also lists all the rules in a worksheet. This dialog box can be accessed from the **Conditional Formatting** drop-down list on the Ribbon.

The New Formatting Rule Dialog Box

The **New Formatting Rule** dialog box lists six types of conditional formatting rules that you can apply.

Rule Type	Description
Format all cells based on their values	Cells are formatted based on their values. You need to specify the minimum and maximum values for which the formatting needs to be applied. It cannot be used for text data.
Format only cells that contain	Cells are formatted based on their numeric, text, or date type content.
Format only top or bottom ranked values	Used for selecting the top or bottom percentage of cells from the range that will be formatted.
Format only values that are above or below average	Only cells that are above or below the average value are formatted.
Format only unique or duplicate values	Used for applying conditional formatting to cells containing unique or duplicate values.
Use a formula to determine which cells to format	Used for conditionally formatting the cells based on a formula.

The Edit Formatting Rule Dialog Box

The formatting rules can be edited by using the **Edit Formatting Rule** dialog box. To change the formatting criteria, you have to select the rule type and edit the description.

Present PivotTable Data Visually

Procedure Reference: Create a Sparkline

To create a sparkline:

1. Select the data range for which you want to create a sparkline.

2. On the **Insert** tab, in the **Sparklines** group, choose the sparkline type you want to create.

3. In the **Create Sparklines** dialog box, in the **Data Range** text box, enter the range of cells containing the data that the sparklines must be based on, and in the **Location Range** text box, enter the location where you want the sparkline to appear and then click **OK.**

4. If necessary, select a sparkline, and on the **Sparkline Tools Design** contextual tab, in the **Type** group, select the required type of sparkline to change the sparkline type.

Procedure Reference: Group Sparklines

To group a set of sparklines:

1. Select sparklines to be grouped.

2. On the **Sparklines Tools Design** contextual tab, in the **Group** group, click **Group** to group sparklines.

3. If necessary, select any sparkline from the group, and on the **Sparklines Tools Design** contextual tab, in the **Groups** group, click **Ungroup** to ungroup a sparkline.

Procedure Reference: Format Sparklines

To format a sparkline:

1. Select a sparkline or group of sparklines that you want to format.

2. On the **Sparkline Tools Design** contextual tab, in the **Show** group, check or uncheck the required check boxes.

    ● Check or uncheck the **High Point** or **Low Point** check box to show or hide the highest or the lowest value.

    ● Check or uncheck the **First Point** or **Last Point** check box to show or hide the first or the last value.

    ● Check or uncheck the **Negative Points** check box to show or hide negative values.

    ● Check or uncheck the **Markers** check box to show or hide all data markers for a line sparkline.

3. On the **Sparkline Tools Design** contextual tab, in the **Style** group, choose the required style, sparkline color, and marker color to be applied.

Removing Sparklines

To remove a sparkline, select a cell containing sparkline, and on the **Sparkline Tools Design** contextual tab, in the **Group** group, click **Clear.** To delete multiple groups of sparklines, you must select all groups and, from the **Clear** drop-down, select **Clear selected Sparkline Groups.** You can also use the shortcut menu to remove sparklines.

Handling Empty Cells or Zero Values

You can choose how a sparkline handles empty cells in a range by using the **Hidden and Empty Cell Settings** dialog box. The dialog box can be displayed by selecting **Hidden and Empty Cells,** from the **Edit Data** drop-down list, in the **Sparkline** group, on the **Sparkline Tools Design** contextual tab. You can choose to display empty cells through gaps or zeros, or simply connect the existing data series.

Increasing the Size of Sparklines

If a sparkline does not appear clearly due to a large amount of data, you can increase the width of a column or row to enlarge a cell. You can also merge two cells to make a sparkline graphic even bigger.

Procedure Reference: Apply Conditional Formatting

To apply conditional formatting:

1. Select the cell or cells to which you want to apply the formatting.
2. On the **Home** tab, in the **Styles** group, click **Conditional Formatting.**
3. From the **Conditional Formatting** drop-down list, select a conditional format type.

   - Select **Highlight Cells Rules** and from the **Highlight Cells Rules** sub-menu, select a rule. In the displayed dialog box, enter a value for comparison and specify a formatting color to highlight the cells.

   - Select **Top/Bottom Rules** and from the **Top/Bottom Rules** sub-menu, select a rule. In the displayed dialog box, enter a value for the number of values to be formatted and specify a formatting color to be applied to the highest or lowest values in a range of cells.

   - Select **Data Bars** and from the **Data Bars** sub-menu, select a data bar type to display the values as bars of proportional length.

   - Select **Color Scales** and from the **Color Scales** sub-menu, select a color scale to differentiate the data values visually.

   - Select **Icon Sets** and from the **Icon Sets** sub-menu, select an icon set to classify data into three to five categories and apply an icon to each data classification.

Procedure Reference: Create a New Conditional Formatting Rule

To create a new conditional formatting rule:

1. On the **Home** tab, in the **Styles** group, click **Conditional Formatting.**
2. Display the **New Formatting Rules** dialog box.

   - Display the **New Formatting Rules** dialog box using the **Conditional Formatting Rules Manager** dialog box.

     a. Select **Manage Rules.**

     b. In the **Conditional Formatting Rules Manager** dialog box, if necessary, select an option from the **Show formatting rules for** drop-down list to display all rules in a particular location.

     c. Click **New Rule.**

   - Or, from the **Conditional Formatting** drop-down list, select **New Rule.**

3. In the **Select a rule type** section, select the desired option.

    ● Select **2–Color Scale** to compare a range of cells by using a gradient of 2 colors.

    ● Select **3–Color Scale** to compare a range of cells by using a gradient of 3 colors.

    ● Select **Data Bar** to compare the values in a range of cells by representing them as bars of proportional length.

    ● Select **Icon Sets** to classify data into three to five categories and assign an icon to each category.

4. In the **Edit The Rule Description** section, format the cells based on their values.

    ● From the **Format Style** drop-down list, select a format style.

    ● From the **Minimum and Maximum Type** drop-down lists, select **Lowest Value, Number, Percent, Formula,** or **Percentile.**

    ● In the **Minimum and Maximum Value** text boxes, select or enter a value.

    ● From the **Color** drop-down lists, select a color for the minimum and maximum values.

    ● In the **Bar Appearance** section, specify a fill type, fill color, border type, border color, and bar direction.

    ● From the **Icon Style** gallery, select a category to classify the data.

    ● In the **Display each icon according to these rules** section, select a comparison operator, enter a value, and specify the type of data for each icon.

5. Preview the format and click **OK** to apply the new conditional format.

Procedure Reference: Edit an Existing Conditional Formatting Rule

To edit an existing conditional formatting rule:

1. On the **Home** tab, in the **Styles** group, from the **Conditional Formatting** drop-down list, select **Manage Rules.**

2. In the **Conditional Formatting Rules Manager** dialog box, if necessary, select an option from the **Show Formatting Rules For** drop-down list to display all rules in a particular location.

3. In the **Rule** pane, select the rule you want to edit.

4. Click **Edit Rule.**

5. In the **Edit Formatting Rule** dialog box, edit the properties and settings of the rules.

6. Click **OK** to close the **Edit Formatting Rule** dialog box.

7. In the **Conditional Formatting Rules Manager** dialog box, click **OK** to update the rule for the data.

Procedure Reference: Clear a Conditional Formatting Rule

To clear a conditional formatting rule:

1. Select a cell, worksheet, table, or PivotTable with a conditional formatting rule applied.

2. On the **Home** tab, in the **Styles** group, from the **Conditional Formatting** drop-down list, select **Clear Rules,** and from the sub-menu, select an option.

- Select **Clear Rules from Selected Cells** to clear rules from the selected cell.

- Select **Clear Rules from Entire Sheet** to clear rules from the entire worksheet.

- Select **Clear Rules from This Table** to clear rules from the selected table.

- Select **Clear Rules from This PivotTable** to clear rules from the selected Pivot-Table.

ACTIVITY 3-5
Inserting Sparklines

Before you Begin
The My Product.xlsx file is open.

Scenario:
You want to compare sales made by various salespersons in different product categories. You want a visual representation of the comparison, but you do not want any data on the worksheet to be hidden by a chart.

1. Display all the product categories in the flattened PivotTable.

   a. In the Excel window, select the **Product Sales** worksheet.

   b. In the worksheet, click the **Product Category** drop-down arrow, and in the AutoFilter menu, check the **(Select All)** check box and click **OK.**

   c. Observe that all the product categories are displayed in the flattened PivotTable.

   d. Select columns B:E.

   e. On the **Home** tab, in the **Cells** group, from the **Format** drop-down list, select **Column Width.**

   f. In the **Column Width** dialog box, in the **Column width** text box, type *20* and click **OK.**

2. Insert sparklines to display the salesperson-wise sales for each product category.

   a. Select the cell range **B3:B18.**

   b. Select the **Insert** tab, and in the **Sparklines** group, click **Column.**

   c. In the **Create Sparklines** dialog box, in the **Data Range** text box, observe that the data range B3:B18 is specified.

   d. In the **Location Range** text box, type *B20* and click **OK.**

   e. Drag the fill handle to cell E20 to create sparklines for all the product categories.

3. Format the sparklines.

   a. Increase the height of row 20 to display the sparklines clearly.

   b. On the **Sparkline Tools Design** contextual tab, in the **Style** group, click the **More** drop-down arrow, and from the displayed gallery, in the second row, select the second style.

   c. Deselect the sparklines.

   d. Save the workbook.

ACTIVITY 3-6
Apply Conditional Formatting to PivotTable Data

Before You Begin
The My Product.xlsx file is open.

Scenario:
Your organization has decided to reward the best performing salesperson in each product category. In the PivotTable that you have used to display salesperson-wise sales for all product categories, your manager has asked you to highlight the maximum sales value in each category.

---

1. Applying conditional formatting to identify the salesperson with maximum sales in the computers product category.

   a. Select the cell range **B3:B18.**

   b. On the **Home** tab, in the **Styles** group, from the **Conditional Formatting** drop-down list, select **Top/Bottom Rules,** and from the displayed sublist, select **Top 10 Items.**

   c. In the **Top 10 Items** dialog box, in the **Format cells that rank in the TOP** section, in the text box, select **10,** and type **1.**

   d. From the drop-down list, select **Light Red Fill** and click **OK.**

   e. Observe that the cell B7 is highlighted with a light red background because it is the highest sale value in the computers product category.

---

2. Apply the same conditional formatting rule for other product categories.

   a. On the **Home** tab, in the **Clipboard** group, click **Copy.**

   b. Select the cell range **C3:C18.**

   c. On the **Home** tab, in the **Clipboard** group, click the **Paste** drop-down arrow, and from the displayed gallery, in the **Other Paste Options** section, select **Formatting.**

   d. Observe that the cell C9 is highlighted with a light red background because it is the highest sale value in the home appliances product category.

   e. Similarly, apply the conditional formatting for the miscellaneous and mobile phones product categories.

   f. Save and close the workbook.

Lesson 3 Follow-up

In this lesson, you created reports using PivotTables and PivotCharts. Analysis of large volumes of data is simplified through the use of such interactive reports.

1. **How do PivotTables and PivotCharts enhance your report generation skills?**

2. **Which filtering and formatting techniques will you frequently use when working with PivotTables?**

4 | Using DAX Functions in PowerPivot

Lesson Time: 1 hour(s)

Lesson Objectives:

In this lesson, you will use DAX functions in PowerPivot.

You will:

- Manipulate PowerPivot data using DAX functions.
- Extract data from tables.
- Work with time dependent data.

Introduction

You created reports using PivotTable and PivotChart. To add more value to your reports, you may need to manipulate data by extending PowerPivot to enhance its Business Intelligence capabilities. In this lesson, you will use DAX functions to add more information to reports.

The data that is collected may not possess sufficient information for analysis. You may need to manipulate it to aid in data mining. PowerPivot with its advanced DAX functions allows you to manipulate data and improve the effectiveness of your reports.

TOPIC A

Manipulate PowerPivot Data Using DAX Functions

You may have used Excel functions to perform calculations in a worksheet. In addition to the common Excel functions, you will require functions that can handle columns of data in tables. In this topic, you will manipulate PowerPivot data using DAX functions.

The data that you have in tables may not be sufficient for creating reports. You may have to manipulate data and perform calculations to derive the required information. Performing complex calculations using basic formulas may lead to redundant and tiresome entry of formulas. By using various DAX functions, you can arrive at complex results with relative ease and also ensure the accuracy of your data analysis.

Measures

A measure is a formula specifically used in a PivotChart or PivotTable. It can be created only if you add a PivotTable or Pivot Chart to a PowerPivot workbook. A measure, which is evaluated dynamically, provides you with different results depending on the filters applied to a PivotTable. The definition of a measure can contain any arithmetic calculation, including functions.

DAX Functions

Data Analysis Expression (DAX) is an advanced formula language that enables you to create custom calculations in calculated columns of a PowerPivot table and measures in PivotTables. Unlike Excel, PowerPivot includes additional functions for working with relational data and performing dynamic aggregation. DAX functions use tables and columns as arguments.

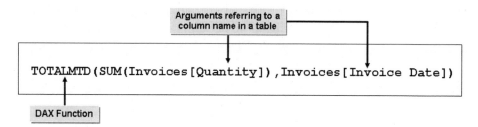

Figure 4-1: *An example of a DAX function used to manipulate data.*

DAX functions are classified under various categories.

Function Category	Description
Date and Time functions	Manipulate date and time values. The functions are similar to Excel date and time functions.
Filter functions	Manipulate the data context by dynamically filtering it in a table or column.

Function Category	*Description*
Information functions	Examine values stored in cells and match them against an expected type.
Logical functions	Validate expressions and values and act upon other data based on the validation.
Text functions	Manipulate textual data. The functions are similar to Excel text functions.
Math and Trigonometric functions	Perform mathematical calculations on data. The functions are similar to Excel math and trigonometric functions.
Statistical functions	Generate statistical results such as count, average, minimum, and maximum values.
Time Intelligence functions	Manipulate data using time periods thereby comparing data across time periods.

Difference between DAX and Excel Functions

DAX functions always refer to a complete column or table, rather than a cell or cell range. DAX functions can return a table as its result, rather than a single value.

Aggregate Functions

An aggregate function takes values in a column as input and provides a single value as the output.

Function	*Description*
AVERAGE	Returns an average of all numbers in a column.
AVERAGEA	Returns an average of all numbers in a column, and it handles both text and nonnumeric values.
COUNT	Counts the number of cells in a column that contain numbers.
COUNTA	Counts the number of cells in a column that are not empty.
MIN	Returns the smallest numeric value in a column.
MAX	Return the largest numeric value in a column.
SUM	Adds all numbers in a column.

How to Manipulate PowerPivot Data Using DAX Functions

Procedure Reference: Use DAX Functions in a Measure

To use DAX functions in a measure:

1. In the Excel window, on the **PowerPivot** tab, in the **Measures** group, click **New Measure** to display the **Measure Settings** dialog box.

2. In the **Measure Name** text box, enter a desired name for the measure.

3. In the **Measure Settings** dialog box, in the **Formula** text box, enter a formula that includes a DAX function.

    ● Type a formula manually.

    ● Enter a formula using the AutoComplete feature.

    ● Insert a formula using the **Insert Function** dialog box.

        a. In the **Measure Settings** dialog box, in the **Formula** section, click **fx.**

        b. In the **Insert Function** dialog box, from the **Select a category** drop-down list, select the desired DAX function category.

        c. In the **Select a function** list box, select the desired DAX function.

        d. Click **OK.**

4. If necessary, click **Check Formula,** to validate the formula that you entered.

5. Click **OK.**

Procedure Reference: Use DAX Functions in a Calculated Column

To use DAX functions in a calculated column:

1. On the PowerPivot worksheet, select a new column, and then click in the Formula Bar.

2. Type a formula containing a DAX function, and press Enter.

ACTIVITY 4-1
Implementing DAX Functions

Data Files:

C:\084606Data\Using DAX Functions in PowerPivot\Products.xlsx

Before You Begin:
The Excel 2010 application is open.

Scenario:
You want to use the PivotTables that you created to analyze the annual sales for the previous years. You want to breakdown the sales performance of each product year-wise, based on which your management can change the marketing strategy of each product.

---

1. Create a calculated column to display the year of sale of a product.

    a. In the Excel window, select the **File** tab, and choose **Open.**

    b. In the **Open** dialog box, navigate to the C:\084606Data\Using DAX Functions in PowerPivot folder.

    c. Select **Products.xlsx** and click **Open.**

    d. Launch the PowerPivot window.

    e. Select the **Add Column** column header and click in the Formula Bar.

    f. Type **=YEAR(Invoice Date[Invoice Date])**

    g. Observe that the year of sale of each invoice is listed in the calculated column.

    h. Double-click the **CalculatedColumn1** column header, type **Year of Sale** and then press **Enter.**

---

2. Modify the PivotTable to display product sales by year.

    a. Switch to Excel, and in the **PowerPivot Field List** pane, click **Refresh.**

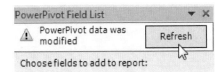

b. In the **PowerPivot Field List** pane, in the **Invoices** section, observe that the **Year of Sale** field is added.

c. Check the **Year of Sale** check box.

d. Observe that the Sum of Year of Sale field is displayed in the **Values** drop zone and drag it to the **Report Filter** drop zone.

e. In the **Report Filter** drop zone, click the **Region** drop-down arrow, and select **Remove Field.**

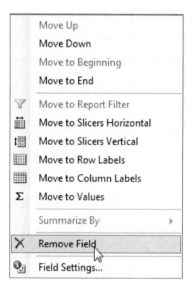

f. In the PivotTable, click the **Year of Sale** drop-down arrow, and in the AutoFilter menu, expand **All,** and check the **Select Multiple Items** check box.

g. Uncheck the **All** check box, check the **2011** check box, and click **OK** to display the 2011 sales for all products.

3. Create a measure to display the maximum product sales that was achieved in each product category during a particular year.

a. On the **PowerPivot** tab, in the **Measures** group, click **New Measure.**

b. In the **Measure Settings** dialog box, in the **Measure Name (All Pivot Tables)** text box, click and drag over the existing text to select the text, and then type *Maximum Sales*

c. Observe that the same name is displayed in the **Custom Name (This PivotTable)** text box.

d. In the **Formula** text box, click and type *MAXA(Invoices[Sales])*

e. Click **Check formula,** observe that there are no errors, and then click **OK.**

f. Observe that the Maximum Sales column displays the maximum sale made in a single invoice for each product, and the maximum of each category in the product category row.

g. Save the workbook as *My Products*

TOPIC B

Extract Data from Tables Using Functions

You manipulated data using various DAX functions. In addition to performing calculations on data, you may need to work with subsets of data. In this topic, you will extract data from tables using DAX functions.

In PowerPivot tables, you may come across situations where you need a part of a table or just specific columns of data. By using DAX functions, you can extract values, columns, or tables which are a subset of the main table to perform complex analysis and thereby enhance the result of data analysis.

Filter Functions

Filter functions return a table, a column, or a value extracted from a table, and look up values in a related table. Using filter functions, you can manipulate data and create dynamic calculations. A few filter functions are commonly used with large data sets.

Function	Description
ALL(table_or_column) *Ignore all slicers*	Returns all rows in a table, or all values in a column, ignoring any filters that might have been applied to a specified table or column.
ALLEXCEPT(table,column1,column2...) *a particular slicer*	Returns all rows in a table after removing all filters except the ones that have been applied to the specified columns.
ALLNONBLANKROW(table_or_column>)	Returns all rows, except for the blank rows, in a table or column, and disregards any filters that might have been applied to a specified table or column.
CALCULATE(expression,filter1,filter2,...) *with columns*	Evaluates the expression after overriding the existing filters for columns specified in the filter arguments and applying the specified filters.
CALCULATETABLE(table_ expression,filter1,filter2,...)	Returns a table of values by evaluating the table expression after overriding the existing filters for columns specified in the filter arguments and applying the specified filters.
DISTINCT(column)	Returns a one-column table that contains distinct values from a specified column.
EARLIER(column,number)	Returns the current value of a specified column in an outer evaluation pass of the mentioned column.
EARLIEST(table_or_column)	Returns the current value of a specified column in an outer evaluation pass of the mentioned column, but lets you specify an additional level of recursion.

Function	*Description*
FILTER(table,filter)	Returns a table that is a subset of a specified table extracted by applying a filter to it.
FIRSTNONBLANK(column,expression)	Returns the first non-blank values in column, filtered by expression.
RELATED(column)	Returns a single related value for the current row from a specified column in another table.
RELATEDTABLE(table)	Returns a table that contains all rows that are related to the current row from a specified table.
VALUES(column)	Returns a one-column table that contains distinct values from a specified column. This function is similar to the DISTINCT function, but the VALUES function can also return an unknown member from a related table.

How to Extract Data from Tables Using Functions

Procedure Reference: Use a Filter Function in a Calculated Column

To use a filter function in a calculated column:

1. In the PowerPivot window, select a new column, and then click in the Formula Bar.
2. Type a formula containing the desired filter function and press Enter.

Procedure Reference: Use a Filter Function in a Measure

To use a filter function in a measure:

1. Display the **Measure Settings** dialog box.
2. Specify a name for the measure and in the **Formula** text box, enter the formula containing the desired filter function.
3. If necessary, click **Check Formula** to validate the formula.
4. Click **OK** to close the **Measure Settings** dialog box.

ACTIVITY 4-2
Extracting Data Using DAX Functions

Before You Begin:

The My Products.xlsx file is open.

Scenario:

The success of your company's performance has instilled new vigor and intensity in your manager. He has planned to execute a major revamp of your organization, for which he wants you to calculate the sales performance of the past few years. You need to analyze the category-wise sales performance of each product and arrive at the percentage share of each product within a category.

1. Restructure the PivotTable.

   a. Verify that the PivotTable in the Sales Report worksheet is displayed, and in the **PowerPivot Field List** pane, in the **Choose fields to add to report** list box, in the **Invoices** section, uncheck the **Maximum Sales** check box.

   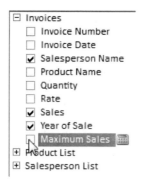

   b. In the **Report Filter** drop zone, click the **Year of Sale** drop-down arrow, and select **Remove Field.**

2. Create a measure which displays the sum of sales based on the category.

   a. On the **PowerPivot** tab, in the **Measures** group, click **New Measure.**

   b. In the **Measure Settings** dialog box, in the **Table name** text box, observe that **Invoices** is displayed.

   c. In the **Measure Name (All PivotTables)** text box, click and drag over the existing text, and then type **Categorywise Sales** to name the measure.

   d. In the **Formula** text box, click and type **CALCULATE(SUM(Invoices [Sales]), ALLEXCEPT('Product List', 'Product List'[Product Category]))**

e.   Click **Check formula,** observe that there are no errors, and then click **OK.**

---

3.   Create a measure to display the share of each product in the respective category.

a.   On the **PowerPivot** tab, in the **Measures** group, click **New Measure.**

b.   In the **Measure Settings** dialog box, in the **Measure Name (All PivotTables)** text box, click and drag over the existing text, and then type *Product Share*

c.   In the **Formula** text box, click and type *Invoices[Sum of Sales]/ Invoices[Categorywise Sales]*

d.   Click **Check formula,** observe that there are no errors in the formula, and click **OK.**

---

4.   Change the number format for the product share values to display them as percentages.

a.   Select cell D3, and on the **PivotTable Tools Options** contextual tab, in the **Active Field** group, click **Field Settings.**

b.   In the **Value Field Settings** dialog box, click **Number Format.**

c.   In the **Format Cells** dialog box, in the **Category** list box, select **Percentage.**

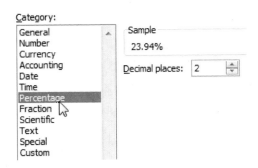

d.   In the right pane, in the **Decimal places** spin box, observe that the number of decimal places is two.

e.   Click **OK** in the **Format Cells** and **Value Field Settings** dialog boxes.

f.   Observe that the values are displayed with two decimal digits and the percentage symbol.

g.   Save the workbook.

TOPIC C
Work with Time Dependent Data

You calculated values based on specific data that you extracted from a table. You may also need to perform calculations on data spread over a period of time. In this topic, you will use DAX functions to work with time dependent data.

When analyzing data, you are bound to come across date and time information. Manipulating such data into meaningful information provides better clarity to your data analysis. DAX functions facilitate such analysis through the use of time intelligence functions that allow you to manipulate data over time periods.

Time Intelligence Functions

Time intelligence functions help you to manipulate data using time periods such as days, months, quarters, and years, and then build and compare calculations over those periods. A few time intelligence functions are frequently used in business intelligence analysis.

≈ START OF MONTH

Function	Description
ENDOFMONTH(date_column)	Returns the last day of the month in a specified date column.
ENDOFQUARTER(date_column)	Returns the last day of the quarter in a specified date column.
ENDOFYEAR(date_column)	Returns the last day of the year in a specified date column.
TOTALMTD(expression,date_column,filter)	Evaluates an expression for an interval that starts from the first day of the month and ends at the latest date in a specified date column.
TOTALQTD(expression,date_column,filter)	Evaluates an expression for an interval that starts from the first day of the quarter and ends at the latest date in a specified date column.
TOTALYTD(expression,date_column,filter)	Evaluates an expression for an interval that starts from the first day of the year and ends at the latest date in a specified date column.
CLOSINGBALANCEMONTH(expression,date_column,filter)	Evaluates the specified expression for the last date of the month. The month is calculated as the month of the latest date in the given date column, after applying the specified filters.
CLOSING BALANCEQUARTER(expression,date_column,filter)	Evaluates the specified expression for the last date of the quarter. The quarter is calculated as the quarter of the latest date in the given date column, after applying the specified filters.
CLOSINGBALANCEYEAR(expression,date_column,filter)	Evaluates the specified expression for the last date of the year. The year is calculated as the year of the latest date in the given date column, after applying the specified filter.

Other Time Intelligence Functions

There are many other time intelligence functions which can be used to analyze time based data.

Functions	Description
LASTNONBLANK(date_column,expression)	Returns the last non-blank value calculated for the expression after evaluating the expression for all values in a column.
DATESINPERIOD(date_column,start_date,number_of_intervals,intervals) DATESBETWEEN(date_column,start_date,end_date)	Returns a table of dates that are found in a specified date column beginning with the start date and continues for the specified number of intervals or ending with the end date.
FIRSTDATE(date_column) LASTDATE(date_column)	Returns the first or the last date in a specified date column.
STARTOFMONTH(date_column) STARTOFQUARTER(date_column) STARTOFYEAR(date_column[<YE_date]	Returns the first day of the month, quarter, or year in a specified date_column.
ENDOFMONTH(date_column) ENDOFQUARTER(date_column) ENDOFYEAR(date_column)	Returns the last day of the month, quarter, or year in a specified date_column.
PREVIOUSDAY(date_column) PREVIOUSMONTH(date_column) PREVIOUSQUARTER(date_column) PREVIOUSYEAR(date_column)	Return the previous date or a set of dates in the previous month, quarter or year from a specified date_column.
NEXTDAY(date_column) NEXTMONTH(date_column) NEXTQUARTER(date_column) NEXTYEAR(date_column)	Returns the next date or a set of dates in the next month, quarter, or year from a specified date_column.
DATESMTD(date_column) DATESQTD(date_column) DATESYTD(date_column)	Returns a subset of dates from the date_column, for an interval that starts from the first day of the month, quarter, or year and ends with the latest date that is specified for a month, quarter, or year.
OPENINGBALANCEMONTH(expression,dates,filter) OPENINGBALANCEQUARTER(expression,dates,filter) OPENINGBALANCEYEAR(expression,dates,filter)	Evaluates the expression at the calendar end of a month, quarter, or year prior to the given month, quarter, or year.
DATEADD(date_column,number_of_intervals,interval)	Returns a table that contains a column of dates, shifted either forward or back from the dates in a specified date_column, by the specified number of intervals. The interval can be specified as year, quarter, month, or day.
PARALLELPERIOD(date_column,number_of_intervals,intervals	It moves the specified number of intervals and then returns all adjacent full months which contain any values after this interval.

How to Work with Time Dependent Data

Procedure Reference: Use Time Intelligence Functions in a Calculated Column

To use time intelligence functions in a calculated column:

1. Select a new column, and click in the Formula Bar.

2. Type the formula containing the desired time intelligence function and press **Enter.**

Procedure Reference: Use Time Intelligence Functions in Measures

To use time intelligence functions in a measure:

1. Display the **Measure Settings** dialog box.

2. Specify a name for the measure, and in the **Formula** text box, enter the formula containing the desired time intelligence function.

3. Click **OK.**

ACTIVITY 4-3
Manipulating Data Over Time Periods

Before You Begin:
The My Products.xlsx file is open.

Scenario:
After analyzing the category-wise information of each product, you now have a fair picture of every products' performance. You then receive a request from your manager to provide the sales figures for the final month and year for which the invoices are available. He plans to use the latest figures to carry out his plans of boosting the company's sale in the next fiscal year.

---

1. Modify the PivotTable.

   a. In the **PowerPivot Field List** pane, in the **Choose fields to add to report** list box, in the **Invoices** section, uncheck the **Sales** and **Categorywise Sales** check boxes, scroll down, and uncheck the **Product Share** check box.

   b. Check the **Quantity** check box.

---

2. Create a measure to display the total sale for the final month.

   a. Select the **PowerPivot** tab, and in the **Measures** group, click **New Measure.**

   b. In **Measure Settings** dialog box, in the **Measure Name (All PivotTables)** text box, select the existing text, and then type **Month to Date**

   c. In the **Formula** text box, click and type **TOTALMTD(SUM(Invoices[Quantity]), Invoices[Invoice Date])** and click **OK.**

---

3. Create a measure to display the total sale for the final year.

   a. On the **PowerPivot** tab, and in the **Measures** group, click **New Measure.**

   b. In **Measure Settings** dialog box, in the **Measure Name (All PivotTables)** text box, select the existing text, and type **Year to Date**

   c. In the **Formula** text box, click and type **TOTALYTD(SUM(Invoices[Quantity]), Invoices[Invoice Date])** and click **OK.**

   d. Save the workbook and close it.

Lesson 4 Follow-up

In this lesson, you manipulated data using DAX functions. Knowing how to use DAX functions will help you to perform complex data analysis and dynamic aggregation with relational data.

1. **Which DAX functions would you commonly use in your analysis?**

2. **Would you prefer to use DAX functions over Excel functions? Why?**

5 Distributing PowerPivot Data

Lesson Time: 20 minutes

Lesson Objectives:

In this lesson, you will distribute PowerPivot Data.

You will:

● Protect reports.

● Save PowerPivot reports in different file formats

Introduction

You created PivotTables and PivotCharts from PowerPivot data. You may want to share your reports with other users. In this lesson, you will distribute PowerPivot data in the form of reports.

Working on an important report for hours will be an exercise in futility if you cannot save it in a format that can be distributed. There are also times when you need to prevent unauthorized users from accessing or modifying a report distributed in the Excel format. By ensuring adequate protection for your reports and publishing both reports and data in accessible formats, you can share information and results of your analysis with key decision-makers.

TOPIC A
Protect Reports

You created PivotTable and PivotChart to analyze data. Reports that contain sensitive information must be protected. In this topic, you will protect reports.

In a work environment, there maybe instances where you need to coordinate with others while working on a confidential report. In such cases, it is important to ensure that only authenticated users access the reports, and data is secure. Excel provides you with options to secure your report.

Workbook Protection

The **Protect Workbook** option in the **Changes** group on the **Review** tab allows you to restrict permission to edit a workbook containing PivotTables and PivotCharts. This option displays the **Protect Structure and Windows** dialog box, which you can use to protect the structure of a workbook and ensure that a workbook window always opens in the same size and position. By protecting the structure of a workbook, you can restrict users from inserting, deleting, renaming, moving, or hiding worksheets in the workbook. Workbooks can be password-protected to ensure that only authorized users can open or modify the contents.

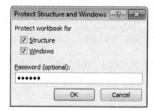

Figure 5-1: *The Protect Structure and Windows dialog box displaying options to protect the layout of a workbook.*

Worksheet Protection

The worksheet protection feature prevents unauthorized users from changing the contents of a worksheet. The **Protect Sheet** dialog box allows you to specify the worksheet element that can be edited by users. To protect PivotTables, the **Use PivotTable reports** check box must be unchecked. If necessary, password protection can be used to prevent unauthorized access.

Figure 5-2: The Protect Sheet dialog box displaying options to protect a worksheet.

How to Protect Reports

Procedure Reference: Protect the Report Structure and Layout of a Workbook

To protect the structure of a report and layout of a workbook:

1. Display the **Protect Structure and Windows** dialog box.

   - In the Excel window, select the **File** tab, choose **Info,** and in the **Permissions** section, from the **Protect Workbook** drop-down list, select **Protect Workbook Structure.**

   - On the **Review** tab, in the **Changes** group, click **Protect Workbook.**

2. In the **Protect Structure and Windows** dialog box, in the **Protect workbook for** section, check the desired check boxes.

   - Check the **Structure** check box to restrict users from adding, editing, or deleting worksheets.

   - Check the **Windows** check box to ensure that a window always opens in the same size and position.

3. If necessary, specify a password to unprotect a workbook.

   a. In the **Password (optional)** text box, type a password so that authorized users can unprotect a workbook for modification.

   b. In the **Confirm Password** dialog box, in the **Reenter password to proceed** text box, retype the password and click **OK** to confirm it.

Procedure Reference: Password Protect a Workbook

To protect a workbook from being opened:

1. Open a workbook you want to protect.

2. On the **File** tab, choose **Save As.**

3. In the **Save As** dialog box, navigate to the folder in which you want to save the file and specify a name for the file.

4. From the **Tools** drop-down list, select **General Options.**

5. In the **General Options** dialog box, in the **File Sharing** section, specify a password to open or modify a workbook.

   - In the **Password to open** text box, type a password to open a file.

   - In the **Password to modify** text box, type a password to modify a file.

6. Click **OK** and confirm the password to open or modify.

   ● In the **Confirm Password** dialog box, in the **Reenter password to proceed** text box, retype the password and click **OK.**

   ● In the **Confirm Password** dialog box, in the **Reenter password to modify** text box, retype the password to modify the file and click **OK.**

7. In the **Save As** dialog box, click **Save** to save the file.

Procedure Reference: Password Protect a Worksheet

To protect worksheets:

1. On the **Review** tab, in the **Changes** group, click **Protect Sheet.**

2. If necessary, in the **Protect Sheet** dialog box, in the **Password to unprotect sheet** text box, type a password.

3. In the **Protect Sheet** dialog box, in the **Allow all users of this worksheet to** list box, check the tasks you want to allow users to perform and click **OK.**

4. If necessary, retype your password for confirmation and click **OK.**

5. Click **OK** to close the **Protect Sheet** dialog box and save the settings.

ACTIVITY 5-1
Securing a PivotTable

Data Files:

C:\084606Data\Distributing PowerPivot Data\Products.xlsx

Before You Begin:
The Excel 2010 application is open.

Scenario:
You created a report using data from PowerPivot. This report contains information regarding product sales in different regions by salespersons. But before distributing it to your coworkers, you want to protect the report from being altered or manipulated.

1. Lock the contents of the Sales Report worksheet.

   a. In the Excel window, select the **File** tab, and choose **Open**.

   b. In the **Open** dialog box, navigate to the C:\084606Data\Distributing PowerPivot Data folder.

   c. Open the **Products.xlsx** file.

   d. Select the **Review** tab, and in the **Changes** group, click **Protect Sheet.**

   e. In the **Protect Sheet** dialog box, in the **Password to unprotect sheet** text box, type a password.

   f. In the **Allow all users of this worksheet to** section, verify that the **Select locked cells** and **Select unlocked cells** check boxes are checked and scroll down.

   g. Observe that the **Use PivotTable reports** check box is unchecked and click **OK.**

   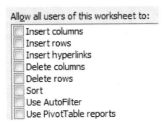

   h. In the **Confirm Password** dialog box, in the **Reenter password to proceed** text box, retype the password and click **OK.**

2. Protect the workbook's structure and windows using a password.

   a. On the **Review** tab, in the **Changes** group, click **Protect Workbook.**

b. In the **Protect Structure and Windows** dialog box, in the **Protect workbook for** section, verify that the **Structure** check box is checked and then check the **Windows** check box.

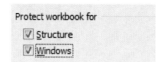

c. In the **Password (optional)** text box, type a password and click **OK.**

d. In the **Confirm Password** dialog box, in the **Reenter password to proceed** text box, retype the password, and click **OK.**

3. Test your settings.

a. In the **PowerPivot Field List** pane, in the **Choose fields to add to report** list box, in the **Invoices** section, check the **Salesperson Name** check box.

b. Observe that the **PowerPivot Field List** pane disappears thereby preventing any changes to the PivotTable.

c. Right-click the **Sales Report** worksheet tab.

d. Observe that the options to insert, delete, rename, move, and hide the worksheet are disabled to prevent any changes to the workbook.

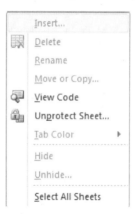

e. Click the Sales Report worksheet tab to close the displayed menu.

4. Verify if users with the password can edit the worksheet.

a. On the **Review** tab, in the **Changes** group, click **Unprotect Sheet.**

b. In the **Unprotect Sheet** dialog box, in the **Password** text box, type the same password used to protect the sheet and click **OK.**

c. Click on the PivotTable to display the **PowerPivot Field List** pane.

d. In the **PowerPivot Field List** pane, in the **Choose fields to add to report** list box, in the **Invoices** section, check the **Salesperson Name** check box.

e. Observe that the quantities sold by Carlos Santos and Joel Marian are displayed in the PivotTable.

f.   On the **Review** tab, in the **Changes** group, click **Protect Workbook** to unprotect the workbook.

g.   In the **Unprotect Workbook** dialog box, in the **Password** text box, type the password used to protect the workbook and click **OK.**

h.   Right-click the **Sales Report** worksheet tab.

i.   Observe that the options to modify the worksheet are now enabled.

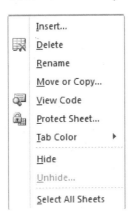

j.   Click the Sales Report worksheet tab to close the displayed menu.

k.   Save the workbook as *My Products*

TOPIC B
Save Reports in Different File Formats

You protected reports from unauthorized access. You may now want to ensure that the reports you created are saved in a format that can be shared. In this topic, you will save reports in different file formats.

You can save PivotTables and PivotCharts in a different format so that users can access it even if they don't have the Excel application or the PowerPivot add-in. Some formats help you to quickly send a file via email or display a report on a website. From PowerPivot, you can publish reports in various formats.

File Formats

Excel provides you with options to save a worksheet in various file formats. Excel data can be saved in formats that allow data sharing, such as the XML, CSV, or text format. PivotTables and PivotCharts can also be saved in platform independent formats such as the PDF or XPS format. You can also save a PivotTable or PivotChart in a format that can be distributed to other users.

The formats in which reports can be saved include common Excel formats and other formats that facilitate data sharing.

Category	File Formats
Excel file formats	• Excel Workbook (.xlsx)
	• Excel Macro-Enabled Workbook (.xlsm)
	• Excel 97–2003 Workbook (.xls)
	• Excel Template (.xltx)
	• Excel Macro-Enabled Template (.xltm)
	• Template (code) (.xltm)
	• Excel Binary Workbook (.xlsb)
	• Excel 97–2003 Template (.xlt)
	• XML Spreadsheet 2003 (.xml)
	• XML Data (.xml)
	• Excel Add-In (.xlam)

Text file formats	• Text (Tab delimited) (.txt)
	• Text (Macintosh) (.txt)
	• Text (MS-DOS) (.txt)
	• Formatted Text (Space-delimited) (.prn)
	• Unicode Text (.txt)
	• CSV (comma delimited) (.csv)
	• CSV (Macintosh) (.csv)
	• CSV (MS-DOS) (.csv)
	• DIF (.dif)
	• SYLK (.slk)
Other file formats	• DBF 3 (.dbf)
	• DBF 4 (.dbf)
	• OpenDocument Spreadsheet (.ods)
	• PDF (.pdf)
	• XPS Document (.xps)

How to Save Reports in Different File Formats

Procedure Reference: Save a PivotTable or PivotChart in the PDF or XPS Format

To save a PivotTable or PivotChart in the PDF or XPS format:

1. Select the worksheet tab that contains the PivotTable or PivotChart that is to be saved.

2. Select the **File** tab, and choose **Save As.**

3. In the **Save As** dialog box, from the **Save as type** drop-down list, select the **PDF** or **XPS Document** format.

4. If necessary, in the **Optimize for** section, select an optimization option.

   • Select the **Standard (publishing online and printing)** option to create a document that is suitable for printing and for online display.

   • Select the **Minimum size (publishing online)** option to create a document that is suitable only for online display.

5. If necessary, click **Options** and in the **Options** dialog box, specify the desired options.

   a. In the **Page range** section, select an option to specify a page range or to print all pages.

   b. In the **Publish what** section, select an option to specify whether a selection, the current worksheet, the entire workbook, or a table is to be published.

   c. In the **Include non-printing information** section, check the desired check boxes to include document properties, and accessibility tags in the published document.

   d. In the **PDF options** or **XPS Document options** section, specify the desired settings.

   e. Click **OK.**

6. If necessary, check the **Open file after publishing** check box to automatically open the published file.

7. Click **Save** to save the file.

Procedure Reference: Publish PowerPivot Data in Different Formats

To publish PowerPivot data in different formats:

1. Launch the PowerPivot window.

2. In the PowerPivot window, select the File tab, and from the displayed list, select **Publish.**

3. If necessary, in the **Save As** dialog box, navigate to the desired location where you want to publish the data.

4. In the **Save As** dialog box, in the **File name** text box, specify a name for the file.

5. From the **Save as type** drop-down list, select the desired file format.

6. Click **Save** to publish the PowerPivot data to the desired folder.

ACTIVITY 5-2
Saving Reports in Other File Formats

Before You Begin
The My Product.xlsx file is open.

Scenario:
Your manager wants to review the reports that you created. It may be difficult for him to access the file because he does not have Excel installed on his system. So, you want to save the report in a format that he can view. You have also been asked to submit the charts that you created in a format that can be shared with the sales team.

---

1. Save the sales charts in PDF format.

   a. In the Excel workbook, select the **Sales Chart** worksheet tab.

   b. Select the **File** tab and choose **Save As.**

   c. In the **Save As** dialog box, in the **File name** text box, type *My Sales Chart*

   d. From the **Save as type** drop-down list, select **PDF (*.pdf).**

   e. In the **Optimize for** section, verify that the **Standard (publishing online and print-ing)** option is selected, and also verify that the **Open file after publishing** check box is checked, and then click **Save.**

   f. Observe that the sales charts are saved in the PDF format and the file is opened in Adobe Reader.

   g. Close the Adobe Reader window.

---

2. Save the workbook in the XPS document format.

   a. Select the **File** tab and choose **Save As.**

   b. In the **Save As** dialog box, in the **File name** text box, type *My Chart*

   c. From the **Save as type** drop-down list, select **XPS Document (*.xps).**

   d. In the **Optimize for** section, verify that the **Standard (publishing online and print-ing)** option is selected, and also verify that the **Open file after publishing** check box is checked and then click **Options.**

e. In the **Options** dialog box, in the **Publish what** section, select the **Entire workbook** option and click **OK.**

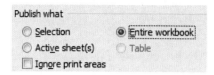

f. In the **Save As** dialog box, click **Save.**

g. Observe that the saved workbook is opened in XPS Viewer.

h. Close the XPS Viewer window.

i. Save and close the workbook and close the application.

Lesson 5 Follow-up

In this lesson, you distributed PowerPivot data. Protecting data and publishing it in an accessible format ensures that your effort is not wasted, and the information is shared with other users.

1. **In which file formats would you publish PowerPivot data?**

2. **How do you use the protection features in Excel?**

Follow-up

In this course, you used PowerPivot add-in to import data from various sources, manipulated it, and applied DAX functions to create a more dynamic report. By familiarizing yourself with the PowerPivot interface, you will be able to create meaningful reports that will aid you in making important business decisions.

1. **Why would you choose PowerPivot for data analysis over Excel 2010?**

2. **Under what situations will you use a PivotChart?**

3. **For what calculations would you use a DAX function?**

What's Next?

After completing this course, you might want to take any one of a number of courses focusing on various applications in the Microsoft Office 2010 suite.

Lesson Labs

Lesson labs are provided as an additional learning resource for this course. The labs may or may not be performed as part of the classroom activities. Your instructor will consider setup issues, classroom timing issues, and instructional needs to determine which labs are appropriate for you to perform, and at what point during the class. If you do not perform the labs in class, your instructor can tell you if you can perform them independently as self-study, and if there are any special setup requirements.

Lesson 1 Lab 1

Exploring PowerPivot Interface

Activity Time: 10 minutes

Data Files:

enus_084606_01_1_datafiles.zip, C:\084606Data\Getting Started With PowerPivot\ Manufacturing Cost.txt, C:\084606Data\Getting Started With PowerPivot\Personnel.accdb, C:\084606Data\Getting Started With PowerPivot\Product Shipping.xlsx, C:\084606Data\Getting Started With PowerPivot\Q1 Sales.xlsx

Before You Begin:

Open the Excel 2010 application.

Scenario:

You have received data from various departments and in various formats. You want to import the data into PowerPivot and analyze it later.

---

1. Open the Q1 Sales.xlsx filefrom the C:\084606Data\Getting Started With PowerPivot.

---

2. Create a linked table using the data in the **Quarterly Sales Calculation** worksheet.

---

3. Change a value in the International column and verify that the change reflects in the PowerPivot window.

---

4. Import the Manufacturing Cost.txt file with the first row as the column header and with tabbed column separators.

---

5. Import both the tables from the Personnel.accdb Access database.

---

6. Import data from the Shipping.xlsx file with the first row as column headers.

---

7. Save the file as **My Imported Data.xlsx** and close it.

Lesson 2 Lab 1

Managing PowerPivot Data

Activity Time: 10 minutes

Data Files:

enus_084606_02_1_datafiles.zip, C:\084606Data\Manipulating PowerPivot Data\Business Data.xlsx

Scenario:

The imported data is raw without any proper formatting applied. You have to present a report next week. To create a detailed and well-organized report, you need to manipulate the data in the worksheet and establish the necessary relationships.

1. Open the Business Data.xlsx file from the C:\084606Data\Manipulating PowerPivot Data folder.

2. In the PowerPivot window, rename the Table 1 worksheet to **Q1 Sales.**

3. In the Manufacturing Cost worksheet, create a calculated column named **Total Cost** to display the sum of the values in the Material Cost and Labor columns.

4. Create a calculated column named **Profit** that displays the total cost deducted from the sales value.

5. Apply the **Currency** format to the Total Cost and Profit columns.

6. Hide the **Region** column in the PowerPivot window.

7. Adjust the column width to display the data in all columns.

8. In the **Orders** worksheet, filter the Product Name column to display any three products of your choice.

9. Sort the data in the worksheet by the Required Date column.

10. Create a relationship between the **Employees** and **Pay and Benefits** tables using **EmpID** as the key column.

11. Save the worksheet as *My Business Data* and close it.

Lesson 3 Lab 1

Analyzing Data Using Reports

Activity Time: 15 minutes

Data Files:

enus_084606_03_1_datafiles.zip, C:\084606Data\Creating PowerPivot Reports\Performance Report.xlsx

Scenario:

A manager wants you to review the sales data for the previous year. As the available data is huge, it will be difficult to make a proper interpretation. To present data in an understandable way, you may have to make use of various functions in Excel.

1. Open the Performance Report.xlsx file from the C:\084606Data\Creating PowerPivot Reports folder.

2. Launch the PowerPivot window.

3. Insert a PivotTable in the Sales worksheet to compare the quantity of products sold by various salespersons by adding the **Company Name, Salesperson, Product Name,** and **Quantity** fields to the PivotTable.

4. Insert a flattened PivotTable in the Quantity of Sales worksheet to display the quantity of each product sold in every country.

5. In the flattened PivotTable, apply filters to view country-wise sales for various products.

6. Insert a PivotChart in the Sales Chart worksheet to compare the sales quantity of each product by different salespersons.

7. Insert a slicer for the PivotChart to apply filters to different products.

8. In the Sales worksheet, apply conditional formatting in column B to highlight values greater than 40.

9. Save the file as *My Performance Report* and close it.

Lesson 3 Lab 2

Analyzing Data with PivotTables and PivotCharts

Activity Time: 15 minutes

Data Files:

C:\084606Data\Creating PowerPivot Reports\Crossword_Starter.html, enus_084606_03_2_
datafiles.zip

Scenario:

In this activity, you will analyze data with PivotTable and PivotChart. It is essential that you complete this lesson to successfully perform the crossword.

1. Complete the crossword provided in the Crossword_Starter.htm document.

2. Check your answers with the Crossword_Solution.htm file provided in the Solution folder.

Lesson 4 Lab 1

Implementing DAX Functions

Activity Time: 10 minutes

Data Files:

enus_084606_04_1_datafiles.zip, C:\084606Data\Using DAX Functions in PowerPivot\
Analysis.xlsx

Scenario:

You have a meeting to discuss the performance of salespersons. Before going to the meeting, you skim through your report and find that some more information can be added to make the presentation impressive.

1. Open the Analysis.xlsx file from the C:\084606Data\Using DAX Functions in PowerPivot folder.

2. In the PowerPivot window, in the Invoices worksheet, create a calculated column named **Month** to display the month from the Shipped Date column.

3. Create a calculated column named **Year** to display the year from the Shipped Date column.

4. Insert a PivotTable in an existing worksheet with the **Company Name** and **Salesperson** fields.

5. Create a measure named **Average Sale** with the formula **AVERAGE(Invoices[Sales])** to calculate the average sales made by each salesperson.

6. Create a measure named **Total Sale** with the formula **CALCULATE(SUM(Invoices-[Sales]))** to calculate the total sales made by each salesperson.

7. Format the values in the Average Sale and Total Sale columns to display values in the currency format with two decimal places.

8. Create a measure named **QTD Sale** with the formula **TOTALQTD(SUM(Invoices[Quantity]),Invoices[Order Date])** to calculate the sales by a salesperson in the last quarter.

9. Save the worksheet as **My Analysis** and close it.

Lesson 5 Lab 1

Inserting a PivotTable

Activity Time: 10 minutes

Data Files:

enus_084606_05_1_datafiles.zip, C:\084606Data\Distributing PowerPivot Data\Sales Report.xlsx

Scenario:

To conduct a performance appraisal, you have to generate reports to show the trend in sales during the last fiscal year. Since the report is highly confidential, you may have to lock the file to prevent unauthorized access. The file must be saved in various file formats so that it can be easily accessed using other applications.

1. Open the Sales Report.xlsx file from the C:\084606Data\Distributing PowerPivot Data folder.

2. Password protect the PivotTable in the Sales worksheet to restrict unauthorized modification.

3. Protect the workbook structure.

4. In the Sales Chart worksheet, save the PivotChart as a PDF document named *My Product Chart*.

5. Save the entire workbook as an XPS document named *My Sales Data*.

6. Save the worksheet as *My Sales Report* and close it.

Glossary

calculated column
A column which has values calculated from values in other columns.

conditional formatting
Conditional formatting is a technique used to format a specified cell or selected range of cells in a PivotTable

connection
A data link created between a PowerPivot workbook and a data source.

data feeds
A mechanism that allows users to receive frequently updated content from a data source.

data refresh
The process of updating the imported PowerPivot data to reflect changes made in the source data.

DAX
(Data Analysis Expression) A formula language that provides functions to perform calculations in PowerPivot.

flattened PivotTable
A PivotTable which is used to categorize data into groups and represent it in the form of a table.

Formula Bar
A bar located below the Ribbon, that allows you to enter and edit cell values.

linked table
An Excel table that is linked to and shares data with a PowerPivot table.

measures
a column of values in an Excel worksheet which are defined by a DAX function.

navigation bar
A bar located below the worksheet, that allows you to navigate through the sheets in the workbook.

PivotChart
An interactive chart that graphically represents the data in a PivotTable report.

PivotTable
An interactive worksheet table used to summarize large amounts of data and view relationships between various fields.

PowerPivot
An Excel add-in that is used to import data from various sources and analyze the data.

Quick Access toolbar
A toolbar that provides access to frequently used commands.

Ribbon
A panel that provides access to various commands.

slicer
A tool that allows you to apply filters in a PivotTable or PivotChart.

sparklines

Tiny charts which are embedded in a cell to represent a trend for specified range.

time intelligence

A category of DAX functions that allow you to manipulate and compare data over a specified period of time.

title bar

A bar located at the top of the application window that displays the name of the document.

worksheet area

The area below the Formula Bar, that encloses the table data.

Index